# Walk In Pieces-
## Diary of a Krav Maga Practitioner

## Lance Manley

© Copyright 2015, Lance Manley

The moral right of the author has been asserted.

# Also by Lance Manley:

- Stab Proof Scarecrows
- Cowboy
- Alaskadie and the Seal of Rock & Roll
- The Cockroach Effect (with Diana Aquino)
- Warlord and Twinkle
- Two Princes

# As LR Manley:

*The Tales of Alegria-*

1). The Catastrophe of the Emerald Queen

2). The Sunder of the Octagon

# Dedications

To my father Mike, a black belt in Judo and the first and greatest badass I ever met.

# A Brief History of Krav Maga

Krav is a self-defense system (NOT a martial art) developed for the Israeli armed forces. It is comprised of a wide range of styles and techniques from Judo, boxing, Aikido and wrestling along with pragmatic fight instruction. Krav Maga is recognised for its focus on realistic circumstances and particularly efficient and brutal counter-attacks.

It came from street-fighting skills created by Hungarian-Israeli martial artist Imi Lichtenfeld, a trained boxer and wrestler as a way to defend the Jewish quarter against fascist factions in Bratislava, Czechoslovakia in the 1930s.

In the 1940s, in Israel, Imi began to provide lessons in combat to what later became the IDF. They later went on to expand the methods that became known as Krav Maga. Since then it has been developed for military, police and civilian roles.

Krav Maga has a viewpoint stressing simultaneous defensive and offensive maneuvers, threat neutralization and aggression. Closely related variants have been adopted by law enforcement and intelligence organizations, Mossad and Shin Bet.

The name in Hebrew can be translated as "contact combat". The root word krav (קרב) means "combat" and

and maga (מגע) means "contact".

Krav Maga primarily encourages students to avoid confrontation. If this is impossible or dangerous, it encourages concluding a fight as fast as possible. Attacks are aimed at the most vulnerable parts of the body, and training is not restricted to techniques that steer clear of severe injury.

Being aware of surroundings while dealing with threats in order to look for escape routes is fundamental. Also additional attackers, items potentially useful to defend or help attack, etc. Another aspect of Krav Maga is learning to be aware of the psychology of a "street altercation", identifying budding intimidation prior to a possible attack. It may also cover ways to deal with physical and verbal methods to avoid violence whenever possible.

# Foreword

Since 2010 I have practiced Krav Maga. Initially with Krav Maga Roma in Italy and currently with Krav Maga Midlands (KMM), a UK club.

I wasn't, haven't been, and am still not someone who enjoys fighting. I'm not very good at it and what attracted me to Krav Maga was that it is above anything else, brutally and unashamedly direct. Forget "respect your opponent" or "fighting fair", Krav for me was what I'd never found in traditional martial arts. It teaches pragmatism, resourcefulness and most importantly, that your ego is nothing more than a spoiled child who needs to be reined in occasionally and sent to the naughty step. Your ego might in fact get you killed.

As a non-fighter but not a coward I had, in the days before I took up Krav, stood my ground in order to prove that I wasn't a wimp...even when doing that might have been a tad silly. That mindset had put me in situations where I could have been hospitalised or even killed.

I'm a former English police officer (both Special and Regular Constabulary) and UK cops in my era (2004+) if faced with an aggressive person, were taught to push to the chest with both hands, shout "GET BACK!!!" and then reach for their baton or pepper spray when subduing a violent suspect. This means it will take up to six cops to arrest one guy who's physically reluctant to spend the night in a cell.

When I took up Krav it showed that being "sensible" was nothing to be ashamed of. Instructors will always tell you during knife disarm training that compliance or "the least creative option" is the way to go.

However, you ALWAYS need a Plan B to fall back on if that isn't going to be enough to save you from getting hurt. Krav Maga does not say that after training regularly you will be able to whup a bad guy's ass. But it does say, "Here's more tools than you had before. Choose which one will help you." It works on techniques that are adaptable and open to anybody with the self confidence to stick up for themselves. In my club we have a guy pushing 60 and two 16 year old girls with a lot of ages spread between them.

This isn't a "How to" manual. Neither is it a book that illustrates overcoming obstacles as you race towards Expert level. It's my views and feelings on Krav Maga and my own personal take on what I've done in the few years I've been training. Krav has been something that's increased my confidence whilst deflating my ego. It's made me a lot less paranoid and helped me to approach situations in many areas of my life with calm.

Most of it comes from my online blog, Krav Maga Practitioner, which also has a Facebook group.

There are some things "missing" from the book such as an account of my P1 grading or the early days. This is because I never wrote about them at the time, and it would be cheating to retrospectively do them now just to make the book more complete. What you read is how I felt then, not now.

There are also interviews in here from an ongoing (yet irregularly updated) series called "Unique Practitioners", and two short, fictional stories involving parents protecting their children.

Enjoy, and see you in training maybe.

Lance Manley- KMG UK
October 2015

kravmagapractitioner.blogspot.com

# Davina & Goliath

2nd February 2013

At Krav Maga there are some big lads. I don't just mean big lads. I mean dudes weighing 17 to 20 stone. BIG guys who are in the higher grades and have done various martial arts for many years. We have classes twice a week and they mainly cover techniques, with drills of those techniques at the end of the class.

However...

On a Thursday night we do Combat after the main session. An hour of full on sparring and kicking, mixed with further technique work.

I have a phobia of being punched aggressively. Always have. I did this class for the first time about 8 months ago and was extremely uncomfortable during and after the session. We wear full head helmets, shin guards, forearm guards, groin guards, 16oz boxing gloves and gum shields. We are protected but when the instructor splits us into pairs and says "OK go!" you protect your head and try and punch hell out of the other guy. Then those words, like nails down a blackboard are uttered; "SWITCH PARTNERS!!!" Here we move to the nearest other person BUT you don't know who you're going to get.

They could be big, small, male, female, experienced or

novice. Then off you go again.

It took me about 6 months to get used to this class and, like a phobia of spiders, I still get nervous sometimes when I decide to stay the extra hour once most people are packing up their kit bags in the trunks of their cars after session 1.

However...

Tonight a 16 year old girl decided to stay for the first time at the Combat session. She started the classes when she was still 15 and is always happy and smiling, even when knackered after a heavy workout. I suggested she stay on and the instructor said OK. As we got into the physical contact I wondered how she'd cope and one inventive scenario had us stand in a circle with our arms outstretched wearing boxing gloves. Guy in the middle had to throw punches to the hands of one person (who couldn't retaliate) BUT anyone behind or to the side of that person could throw a punch to make them turn around. Doubly so if the guy had dropped his guard and had left his face or head exposed.

I was first up and it was exhausting. Shouting, some encouragement and cries of "COME ON! HARDER!" Disorientating, scary and tiring. It only lasted a minute but felt a lot longer. My arms felt like lead and having to hold them out for the others to hit after, was doubly aching.

We worked our way through one at a time and then it was the 16 year old girl's turn.None of us lay into her the way we had each other but she took it all in her stride and to my pleasant surprise threw a last burst of energy into the final few seconds, giving it her all.

The final 5 minutes was full on sparring so we helmeted up. The instructor said to her "You can sit this one out."

She looked at him and said curiously "Why can't I join in?"

After a pause he replied "You don't have the equipment yet. You can watch."

We then had a glorious time knocking the hell out of each other and at the end as I pulled my sweaty gloves off and yanked the helmet from my head with a sodden tug I waited for my breathing to return to normal and then asked her "Now you've seen that, would you have still wanted to do it?"

She beamed and went "Yes, if I'd had the same equipment as you all."

If a 16 year old, 5 feet 4 inch girl can fight with a room of guys aged between 22 and 42, of varying sizes and ability, and simply regard it all as F.U.N.....then the moral is....

Courage is from the soul, not the body.

# Sticks & Stones (& Knives & Guns & Bottles) Will Break My Bones
# Krav Maga Midlands- Armed Attacker Seminar

Saturday, 16th February 2013

Saturday 16th of February was the Armed Attacker seminar. UK Krav is not predominantly based on guns, due to the lack of them in general street crime. As a result we focus mainly on knife attacks in classes. After all, the average Chav mugger has free and easy access to his mother's cutlery drawer, but finds it harder to get hold of something that fires bullets.

Knowing this seminar had sold out a week or two in advance I was keen to attend and try a different side of Krav Maga.

First of all, it was great to see people from other clubs. I chatted to a couple of guys who had come from the south of England, one from London and the other Bristol. I also got to meet members of the other Krav Maga Midlands groups, which was cool as we rarely interact apart from the occasional social event or when people borrow another group, either due to missing their regular session or taking Option 3 on the payments scheme (the right to attend any and all classes that KMM holds in a week).

Have to say that the warm-up brought out the kid in me. So much fun chasing around a huge sports hall along with 50 other people, playing Tig. After that brief burst of cardio, we cracked straight on with knife attacks. This was something we'd covered in classes but it was good as it put some shine on the rust and meant we slid straight into it. The much larger space to train in was appreciated. While Krav teaches you to fight and defend in ANY space, be it confined or vast, it's good to know you won't be smacking the back of your head into the pair training behind you (although I've no doubt that would be blamed on me neglecting to scan after defending!)

After that we moved to 4 feet-long sticks. Thankfully the wooden sticks we used had foam sheathing but still gave a whack if you got them across the head or forearms. This was my favourite part of the seminar, as there is something immensely satisfying about taking a big stick off someone determined to thump you with it. My partner was annoyed that I wouldn't release the stick unless he actually made me and mimed kicking my knee cap, saying "If I kicked you there, you'd let it go!

I replied "Yes, but you're NOT kicking me there. Adapt!"

The best one of this whole section of training was the move that meant you forced your assailant's arm up behind his back by twisting the stick, and put him on his knees.

It is quite fiddly to do properly, but brutally effective if done right.

Finally we did gun disarm training. Personally I'm hesitant about this, as I believe you have to be VERY calm and sure of your abilities to even dream of thinking about taking a pistol off someone, let alone one being pointed in your face. However, Bartosz partially covered some of this, saying that some guy pointing a gun at you in the street is probably assuming you will do what he wants just because he is holding the pistol and won't expect an unarmed "victim" to attack.

My other phobia on this one was the fact that the dummy guns were pistols with slides on the top. The disarm move taught us to grab the top of the gun and twist it away while stepping clear.

I had evocative images of a real pistol in a real situation, accidentally firing in the struggle and breaking at least one of my fingers as the slide activated. Bartosz again covered this aspect, without anyone asking him, by saying that if you grip the top of the gun and the trigger is pulled, then the gun will jam and have to be cleared and reloaded before it can be used.

Nicest part of the whole thing was finding out that if you take a pistol off someone properly, there's a fair chance you will break their index finger as it's going to be trapped in the guard.

Needless to say we threatened each other with fingers WELL clear of the dummy pistol's trigger guard.

To round up, we had a pressure drill of one guy attacking a strike shield held by another student....while three or four guys came at him with a gun, a knife, a stick or a bottle (as the bottle moves are the same as for sticks or knives). I was in a group of six where me and a couple of other blokes made a point of throwing the weapons away from us once we got them off the attacker. Made me smile when one or two people handed them back politely, then carried on punching the bag waiting for the next attack.

One thing I didn't expect was the attendance certificates being awarded one at a time. We lined up against the wall and the names were called out with guys walking up and getting a round of applause from us, and a handshake off Bartosz and Russell. A nice touch and the perfect way to end this.

Really good day and the best fun I've had at Krav apart from my P1 grading.

Just wish my forearms didn't look like someone's been at them with a steak tenderiser.

# Krav Maga Global Practitioner 2 Grading. GMAC, Perry Barr, Birmingham

16th March 2013

After P1 last October I had been forewarned that P2 is P1's older brother and therefore in a different league, i.e. HARDER.

At Reading for P1 we had about 50 guys doing the grading simultaneously. This time the grading was down the road at a new venue in Birmingham, so no 5.30am alarm calls BUT there were a lot less people, with around twenty doing my level due to the increased options on locations. There's something reassuring about having loads of people besides yourself. Like being at a school disco when you're 12 and don't like dancing, it means that you can try to blend in a little more.

The instructor was an Israeli guy named Moran Laskov who was very focused but friendly. We watched the P1 guys finish and realised just how different this grading would be, as the instructor had made notes for each person and gave them verbal feedback in front of everyone else, which hadn't happened last time. It was good to see guys from KMM get their certificates and we shook their hands before taking to the mat for our turn.

The instructor welcomed us and said that not everyone might pass but to regard the experience not with a heavy heart but instead as an opportunity to improve and as "extra training." After a quick warm up we split into A's and B's. As there was an odd number of guys, me and my partner agreed to take another lad onboard with us. In some ways this made it easier for us (less workout time, time to quickly practice a move) but in others it was harder (alternating focus, breaking off to let the other guy have a turn).

My one weakness during the build up to the grading had been backward rolls. I kept either coming down on my neck (which HURTS!!) or rolling off to the side like a drunken sailor slipping on the deck. I had finally nailed this a couple of days before, with extra training from Bartosz and was relieved when it went smoothly and I didn't go spilling off the mat with my arse in the air, into the P3- 5 guys sitting around the edge waiting for their go.

A touch that I appreciated to the proceedings, was that if the instructor realised that more than a couple of us didn't understand what he wanted us to demonstrate, then he would pause the grading and show us himself.

This happened with both body defences and palm strikes to the groin, the latter of which had him explaining why it hurts so much, as the nerve endings are at the top of the testicles which is why you should aim to hit "up" (we all laughed then but I am clenching now just remembering that).

At the end we had a bit of slow fighting and then sat on the floor dripping sweat to get our feedback. The instructor demonstrated moves he felt that all or most of us needed to improve on (such as blocking a hook punch) and then came The Moment.

I once saw a documentary on TV about the Royal Marines. After grueling assessment over a period of weeks, the candidates sat on three benches in an army sports hall and one at a time a Captain read their names out. The soldiers were not allowed to show any emotion, regardless of outcome and it went like this:

Captain: "Smith?"

(Smith stands up): "Sir?"

Captain: "Fail".

Smith: "Sir". (Sits down again).

Captain: "Jenkins?"

(Jenkins stands up): "Sir?"

Captain: "Pass".

Jenkins: "Sir". (Sits down again).

The instructor warned us that not everyone had passed but again said that we should regard this experience as a positive one and try again if it was us. He added that he himself had failed grades a couple of times on the way up and not to be too downhearted about it.

He finally said that we would be receiving feedback via email from him within a couple of days. This last bit was a nice touch and much appreciated as it is beyond what we either expected or had paid for.

We didn't know who had failed until all the certificates had been awarded. As the names were read out we took the certificate from another guy and shook the instructor's hand, while everyone else clapped. Both the guys in my "pair" got theirs before me. When my name was finally read out I think the air rushed from my lungs with the force of a hurricane.

We then had a quick word with Bartosz and Russell and a couple of photos before heading home.

A positive experience and I can't wait for P3 in October.

# Night Parks/ Third Party Protection Seminar
# Krav Maga Midlands
# RSC Park, Stratford-upon-Avon

Friday 19th July 2013

Having attended the Armed Attacker Seminar last February I was hyped up for attending this one too. Bartosz had promised 3 hours of training in how to protect "loved ones" (or in my case "some girl I might pull in a bar one night") from attack in open spaces such as parks or woodland.

I arrived about 6.30pm and found a lot of guys already there, chatting near the river while Bartosz waited at the gate to shepherd people over. It was mainly club members, with one or two "civilians" thrown in, brought as the hypothetical 3rd parties in need of protection. In all there were about forty of us.

At around 7pm Bartosz and Russell l got us warmed up and then we split into pairs for the initial "protection" training. This consisted of numbering ourselves 1 or 2, then jogging around the lawn. Bartosz would intermittently bellow "ONE!" or "TWO!" and whoever's number was called had to find their significant other, and run to stand as a shield in front of them.

Then we had the always enjoyable "slap other people

on the head" addition. This meant that while jogging around you could hit anyone within reach. A couple of the civvies didn't seem to like this too much but it broke the ice and meant we were nicely warmed up for the main session.

After some stretching we split into groups of 3 and worked on protecting someone from perceived or actual attack from ne'er do wells.

My partners were a fairly muscley guy and a very small woman. While she was totally gung ho with regard to getting stuck in, her technique needed a little work as she was unable to push either me or the other guy out the way.

Eventually she cracked it and we had a lovely time shoving each other around. The Educational Block is something I'd forgotten about but a quick reminder session had me coughing and spluttering. It consists of pushing someone away with the palm of your hand and then pushing your fingers into the soft bit just above the top of their rib cage. Not nice!

Later on we had some amusing themes to work with, one of which was shoving your VIP out the way of an oncoming cyclist or skateboarder careening towards you. Very Indiana Jones.

Then it was "protect the VIP" from actual attack. We had to take it in turns to be Attacker, VIP or Defender.

Punishment for letting the Attacker actually reach the VIP was 5 push ups. We couldn't stop until Bartosz shouted, "Switch!" so a lot of grunting, shoving and headlocks were on display as people tired each other out on the grass.

An interesting variant on this was the "VIP Acting Like An Idiot" scenario. In real life, those who are attacked will usually run or stand still but some get lippy and either try to fight as well, shout and scream or wander around like a headless chicken. The most difficult situation was dealing with the oncoming Attacker while simultaneously trying to keep a protective eye on your VIP who was now strolling round like a loose cannon. Stranglehold techniques were gone through, which aren't as hard to break as I'd imagined, albeit somewhat complicated with regard to what arm goes where. Imagine a Chinese puzzle but with human limbs instead of wood or string.

After a 5 minute break we then moved on to knife and gun attacks and how to disarm an attacker. Golden rule of training for pistol disarm is NEVER put your finger in the trigger guard…unless you want it broken when your partner twists it out of your hand. Funniest thing was that 4 police officers wandered through the park just as Bartosz was demonstrating by pointing the fake gun at Russell.

Luckily it's bright yellow (as are 90% of the training pistols) so they didn't take cover behind trees and push the panic alarms on their Airwave radios for an Armed

Response unit to attend.

We then had another quick break and got stuck in to protection against knife, gun or strangling techniques on a pressure drill. This was hard as you had to walk to the left of your partner and attempt to disarm or avoid anyone who was "armed" coming at you. As all 40 of us were in one small area it was very intense but a lot of fun.

While we were getting ready a drunken Chav with a rather flabby belly had wandered up and stood near to me watching what was going on. His breath reeked of beer and I was starting to get drunk off the passives when Bartosz asked him, "You OK?" He smiled and went, "Yeah, just interested that's all" which was fine until he picked up a fake knife and swung it around saying, "So what would you do if I attacked you with this?" Bartosz snatched the knife off him and shoved him away with an educational block growling, "Just stay away, go!!!" He mooched away with his tail between his legs looking very embarrassed.

This beautiful moment was also caught on film and can be found on You Tube if you search for "Drunk Idiot Removed and Educated."

As it got dark we then had the "surprise" that we'd been promised.

Near the river was a bit of pathway with lots of overhanging trees and dense bushes. Bartosz asked, "Who wants to go first?" and I volunteered. He sent me to stand out of sight while he got 4 or 5 other guys to hide along the path. When he called me back he grinned and went , "Right Lance. Just walk down that path until you come out the other end, OK?"

It was very dark by this point and hard to see. As I set off I saw a guy come bursting out of the bush to my left, I was about to kick him when he shouted, "Alright mate! You got the time?" I relaxed a little, realising this was the Red Herring and said, "Sorry mate no. You gave me a fright jumping out like that!"

Then a female student came at me with a fake knife. I booted her in the groin and took the knife off her, spinning round to find someone crouching in the bushes. I was about to give a pre-emptive kick when I realised it was Bartosz's girlfriend Iwona, who was taking photos. Two more lads then came hurtling towards me shouting threats and swearing. I kicked one of them and pushed the other away, warning them with the fake knife I still had and yelled, "JUST FUCK OFF OK!!!"

Bartosz called time and said I'd done well and to return to the main group round the other side.

As other guys went through one at a time a group of four elderly people wandered up to see what we were doing. They all had baseball caps on with "STREET PASTOR" printed across the front and were working for the local church, offering spiritual advice to people. To my utter delight they came up just as a student went through the "tunnel" who misunderstood the first guy's role in the scenario. It went a bit like this:

Street Pastor: "So what are you doing here then?"

Me: "We're with Krav Maga Midlands, we're learning about how to protect against attacks in the dark. The guys over there are…"

First Guy: "Excuse me mate, you got the time?"

Student: "F**K OFF YOU C**T!!!"

(GRUNTING. STRUGGLING. SOUNDS OF PUNCHES & KICKS. SOMEONE FALLING DOWN. SWEARING. etc.)

The Street Pastors looked horrified until I reassured them that this was just a scenario and Bartosz was walking behind the student to make sure no one got hurt. It then turned out that one of them was a guy I work with (hey, it was dark!) and we shook hands and had a laugh. I'll no doubt be ribbed remorselessly over this on Monday morning.**

Then I had a go as a "bad guy" in the bushes and Bartosz said, "Just abuse and push them."

First guy through was OK, pushing me back and then facing my neighbour who simply stood in his way being a nuisance. The third lad through was a big, Indian bloke and when I shouted, "Think you're f**king hard do you?!!

Come on then!!!" and shoved him, he dropped me with a push kick that sent me on my arse into the bushes.

The last-but-one bloke is a former kickboxer and wanted to have a stand up fight with everyone who tried to "mug" him. This isn't the principle of Krav Maga but was fun to see as he wouldn't back down no matter what was thrown at him.

Finally everyone was done and we gathered with the "civilians" and Russell . Bartosz decided to give one last piece of advice and pulled one guy over and put a fake knife in his hand. He then said:

"A lot of you are trying to take the knife when you see it. If it is only being held, you should do this instead."

He then slapped his knife hand away and booted him in the crotch.

A brilliant night's training and I really hope to do this again soon.

*\*I later found out that Ron Ball, Warwickshire county's Police & Crime Commissioner was with them. Christ knows what he thought of it all.*

# Krav Maga Global (UK)
# Practitioner 3 Grading
# Birmingham Gymnastics & Martial Arts Centre, Perry Bar

October 12th 2013

I had heard various rumors that, after the delights of P1 and its big brother, P2 the grading for my next level, P3 would be H.A.R.D.E.R.

It was big boys' pants time, with 2 guys going for P5 specifically stating that P3 was the most difficult grading they'd taken. This was "the other side of the curve" with the first two gradings merely setting the scene for what was to come.

So, with nerves a-jangling and my Sat Nav being a petulant brat and sending me the "pretty" way to Perry Bar, I set off on a rainy Saturday morning to face the baptism by fire.

When I got there the P1s were still on the mats and peering through the windows I could see them doing ground sparring under the supervision of Rune Lind, a KMG Expert 4 examiner who I met a year ago on my P1 grading. One fat guy was at the end of his energy levels and simply lay on the floor, on his back gasping for air. Well, he did until Rune poked him repeatedly with his foot and yelled at him to get up.

There were 4 or 5 Krav Maga Midlands students from my class in there and they looked knackered as they came out and shook hands with me and the other guys waiting for the later levels. All had passed which boosted my confidence and we wished the P2 guys well as they marched in to register. Due to some undisclosed problem, the gradings for P4 and 5 had been moved forward to merge with P3.

This wouldn't have been a quandary apart from the fact that it was decided on the day. Frantic text messages were apparently sent out. Scott sent an SMS to our Chief Instructor Bartosz saying "Not sure if I'll make it on time" to which Bartosz simply replied "Drive faster!"

Everyone made it in good time and I watched some of P2 doing their stuff and chatted with Anna who runs Active Krav Maga in Cheltenham and suggested a twinning between them and Krav Maga Midlands. Time will tell. Two people failed P2 which put a slight dampener on the mood. Felt sorry for them but as Bartosz pointed out, there are Expert levels out there who failed at least one grading on their way up the ladder. When we took to the mat we had a quick warm up and were then formally briefed on the differences that I'd heard about, from P2 to this level.

The instructor said that they didn't want people who "collect patches" and that he hoped we were all there as we believed we were ready for it. He then handed us over to Rune who said that the first time he saw us throw a technique he would regard THAT as the one he was assessing, so we'd best make it good. He pointed out that in his opinion a "pass" was something that would work "on the street." He then split us into groups according to our levels, with the 4 guys doing P5 in one corner and us and P4 on the other side.

He asked for slow fighting at the start and I was seriously worried about my energy levels after 10 minutes as I was feeling like shit and gasping for breath.

We then moved onto techniques and worked through the various stuff we'd spent the last few weeks practicing.

I had no problem with kicks and was quite pleased when my partner holding the strike pad went flying a couple of times.

He could kick hard too and it was difficult not to end up sailing back into the chairs around the edge of the mats.

I guessed we wouldn't be given formal water breaks so took the initiative to ask. Rune was a gentleman and said it was fine, cue much glugging of H2O, orange juice or Lucozade before we got stuck in to knife and stick attacks.

Rune had us do the basic techniques then asked us to

try and get the knife off the attacker. I took my partner to the ground and we were squabbling over the blade until it snapped and I sheepishly handed in the broken bits afterwards.

Forward rolls was something I tried briefly but my ropey right shoulder put paid to that. Krav Maga Global have a common sense approach to injuries and we were specifically asked at the start if we had any existing ailments they should know about. I got excused from "jumping over your partner while they kneel down as if impersonating the Pope kissing the airport runway" but managed a couple of rolls. After 2 and a bit hours of hard work, we moved on to the biggest bastard of the session.

Rune told us to put gloves on and said that those of us (including me) who'd only brought MMA as opposed to 16 ouncers, could only punch lightly, even if our opponent had the proper big jobs on. He said to slow fight to start with and then we would move up in tempo.

We were all completely knackered by this point and I had to find reserves of adrenalin that I'd stashed in a hidden bank vault in order to continue.

After a couple of minutes Rune then told us to spar at normal speed with a new partner.

He added that as one had to be on the ground we had to do 10 push ups facing each other, with the winning presser upper getting to choose which one of the pair had to lie on the floor on their back. I won, let my partner go to the mat and then simply held him down in a body hold while he struggled to get up, until Rune shouted "TIME!"

My next partner also lost the push ups, so he went down and again I held him, with Rune stopping by on his rounds to tell us to punch each other as well as just wrestle it out. The guy eventually said, "I have to tap out mate, I can't breathe!" and I stood up and we then moved to stand up scrapping. I was ready to drop dead by this point and went hammer and tongs with the remaining energy I had left. I was reassured by a couple of instructors I didn't know, who cheered me on saying, "That's good, good job, keep going." My partner caught me a right meaty smack in the chops and then muttered "I'm sorry". I replied in a croaking rasp, "Don't apologise, just fight!"

Finally the longest tussle of my life ended and I dragged my soaking carcass to join the others in a line. Rune and another instructor walked up with a big pile of certificates and smilingly asked, "So step forward anyone who thinks they DESERVE to pass!

Me and about 8 others stepped one pace out and they looked at each other and then back at us before Rune said, "Good start. But if you ever test with Eyal Yanilov never let him hear you say 'I think I might pass the test'. That means you have already failed it." All of P3, 4, and 5 had passed and we proudly walked up to get our certificates, dripping sweat and in some cases limping. I shook hands with my technique partner and the guy I'd sparred with. The latter had a busted lip where I'd hit him and when I pointed out that he was bleeding he replied,

"Yeah, I hoped the instructors would stop the fight but no such luck."

Finally a few photos and I peeled one very wet t-shirt off in favour of a fresher dry one, before driving home.

Tremendous yet grueling day and all I can say now is….bring on P4.

# "Come Closer, Very Fast!"
# Krav Maga Global
# The Bus't Up
# Harlow Leisurezone, Essex

1st December 2013

Having missed my own club's last seminar (Krav Maga Midlands's "Warzone" two weeks ago) I was very much looking forward to this one. Organised by Joe Ambrosino of the Institute of Krav Maga UK and featuring Expert level 3 instructor Jacek Walczak, it promised to be a good un.

The basic premise was that we would be trained to defend ourselves on a train or bus, taking into account the close quarters that fighting in such an environment would have, and adapting our techniques accordingly.

The gold plated bonus though (and 50% of the reason that I signed up for it) was that we would get to try the techniques out on each other…on a real London double decker bus.

The 100-ish mile journey to Harlow was fairly smooth and I booked in at the Leisurezone at 11.15am to get my free seminar t-shirt and bung on the ever necessary groin guard.

Once I'd got changed it occurred to me that anyone

seeing all of us in one place (there were over 100 students, with Jacek, 5 or 6 assistant instructors and a paramedic) might think we were coach drivers learning self defence, judging by the cartoon London Red buses on everyone's backs. I was the only one from Krav Maga Midlands in the room but there were loads of other clubs there and I got chatting to a few guys from London and Kent.

We were introduced to Jacek by Joe and had a quick warm up before going into the techniques. All required close proximity to your partner and it was interesting to actually be taught how to headbutt, something I had only seen in reference up to now.

The confined and claustrophobic nature of a fight on a train or bus, means you have to get in fast, hard and brutal to put an invader down. One useful technique was that if an aggressor puts their hand in their pocket you grab the wrist, punch to the face and then lift the hand out with both of your hands, controlling it all the time. Jacek acknowledged that they might actually be reaching for a mobile phone, but added that in an aggressive situation you must assume the worst. He also showed us about shoving someone away and taking control of a knife.

During Jacek's demonstrations, one bloke asked what you could do if trying to take a knife off someone who is standing beyond fist or shoving range.

Jacek shrugged and said "just do this" then booted the

other instructor really hard in the groin.

Cue much laughter and a round of applause.

After about an 90 minutes we were split into two groups and me plus another 50 guys traipsed out to the double decker parked outside. The whole thing reeked of stale beer, which kind of hit the right note as we were about to recreate the average night bus experience in the grottier parts of London at 3am on a Saturday.

We got stuck in doing releases from the side and back strangleholds from a sitting position. Only problem was 50 sweating, struggling bodies on two decks steamed the glass up in about 30 seconds. The scenario was halted for an instruction to open the windows. Cue more laughter. The claustrophobic nature of this type of thing really came to the fore as we had to be aware of the people next to us, ahead of us and behind us at all times.

After a while we then had the surreal pleasure of "Person About To Miss Their Stop" and one at a time barged through everybody else from one end of the bus to the other while they stood in our way.

We then switched with the other 50 and spent the final 40 or so minutes learning how to defend against punches, kicks and knife attacks while sitting. This was something I'd covered in my own club, but it was interesting to utilise the (folding) chairs as a weapon if attacked.

After a raffle and awarding of certificates we wrapped

things up. Jacek got to be JK Rowling for 15 minutes as he sat at a table and we queued up for his autograph on our diplomas, while Joe pleaded with us to leave Jacek alone so he could catch his plane back to Poland. Me and a few others managed to grab him on the way out for photos before he finally escaped.

A cracking day. Many new techniques learned and Jacek is one scary looking, ferocious dude.

I also don't think that I've recently seen anything as surreal as 50 guys in identical t-shirts, attempting to kick the hell out of each other on a London Double Decker bus.

Brilliant!

# Being Bendy

5th February 2014

Tonight at Krav we were doing high kicks. They started off as groin kicks with a side swipe forward leg defence...and the progressed to "What if the person aims for your face or chin instead?"

The block for the higher kick is with the forearm, but the person throwing the kicks has to aim for the face. My opponent was about 6' 3" and I'm about 5' 10".

One thing I've realised as I've got older is that I am not as flexible as a high kick to the chin (especially on some of the giraffe sized blokes that attend the club) would demand.

Tonight was the first time I felt relatively confident attempting these kicks, without wondering if I'd get groin strain or throw my hips out of alignment.

The reason is that 6 weeks ago I started a Yoga class.

The teacher is a mild mannered Korean lady who has an aura of peace and tranquility and told me off for asking "Is my arse meant to hurt this much?" when the correct terminology is apparently "bottom."

The first four lessons were very difficult and I glanced at my (predominantly female) neighbours with some envy as they comfortably assumed the Lotus position when I could barely manage to cross my legs without wincing.

The joyous moment occurred last week when my body finally gave slightly to the manipulations and positions I was putting it through. I was able to lean just a little bit further than I had before.

While Krav Maga and Yoga don't seem on the surface to be good flat mates, the great thing is that I can now kick with more confidence.

By that I mean without that little voice in my head telling me that I'm going to rupture some internal organs.

For the Combat side of Krav, flexibility is a must. Dodging, weaving and ducking under someone else's punches and kicks is hard, doubly so when you are retaliating. Being "loose" is a necessity and the freedom of movement I've so far not had, has finally started to work its way into my stubborn joints

For Practitioners who don't bend so easily I recommend Yoga to help you get freed up and also to reduce the risk of coming home aching, bruised and possibly stiff as a board next morning.

# Want To

6th February 2014

It's not melodramatic to say that when I contemplate staying for combat class, I feel like a child again. I've read some stuff about emotional memory and how experiences as a kid will imprint themselves on the most instinct-protective parts of the brain, as a means of keeping you safe.

This would be fine if it was stuff like touching flames with your fingers or crossing the road without looking. When it becomes "getting hit" or "getting kicked" or even "being glared at sternly before the other two happen" then it's a bit of a pisser. No, in fact it's a lot of a pisser. Especially if it hangs around like a fart in a wetsuit, well into adulthood.

After being used as a punchbag for a lot of my time in Secondary school I have had a multitude of things to try and help get over the bad memories. I've meditated, I've done the Landmark Forum, I've written down the names of those who bullied me and then burnt it, I've visualised them saying sorry, I've even confronted one or two people over their behaviour***. Bottom line is…nothing has so far shifted my amygdala oblongata to get a grip and stop shaking with fear every time the gum shield goes in and the words "Ready? FIGHT!" are uttered from 8.30 to 9.30pm every Thursday.

I realised after I passed Practitioner 3 last October that I'd have to get a grip on this and attend Combat class regularly if I wanted to go any higher.

I was all up for it the first time after Christmas and actually quite enjoyed it.

But at some point when I was asleep Anxiety and Paranoia met up with The Inner Child and had a quiet word.

The best way to compare this is like being about to step on stage in front of your parents for the Xmas Nativity play**** at Primary school. You know even at age 7 that nothing bad will happen but you are so nervous of walking out in mum's dressing gown with a tea towel wrapped round your head to say your lines that you are practically reduced to jelly.

Excusable in a young child.

Kind of sad in a grown man.

When the kicks and punches fly something within me reverts back to being a kid getting chased by thugs at school. I KNOW the guys I'm sparring with are mates. I KNOW that we are padded up and wearing about as much body armour as a bomb disposal expert and I KNOW that the instructor is supervising.

But there is something deep down that imposes masks

upon my fellow practitioners and makes them look scary and spiteful, no matter how much I tell myself otherwise.

My father cured his fear of spiders by making himself touch the biggest spider he could find (as I recall, he said it was half the size of his hand). That cured his arachnophobia completely, but is about as dramatic as you can possibly get re: shock therapy.

Determined to overcome my gripes and annoying panic attacks around a VERY fundamental obstacle to me progressing in Krav I found inspiration last week from an unexpected source. A guy who's only been in the club a couple of months (I've been in nearly 2 years) was itching to try the Combat classes (normally you wait 3 months after joining the club to try them out) and was over the moon when he finally got to go.

Two weeks ago I had to drop my mate off home before I could join in and after clearing it with the instructor I came back 10 minutes into the session to see everyone kitted up and sparring. I felt uneasy and it had in fact taken some effort of willpower to not go home and later lie and say I'd had car trouble. As I looked at everyone I felt like Katniss Everdeen on the pedestal at the beginning of the 74th and 75th Hunger Games*****.

I got my gear on and asked two guys if I could join them.

As I walked up I glanced over to see the new bloke was partnered with the highest qualified fighter in the room (Practitioner Level 5) who also happens to be 6 feet 11 inches tall.

I paid no further thought to this until I got home and on Facebook the guy had posted a status saying how he'd "got the shit kicked out of me" and it was "awesome!" I made a flippant remark about fighting Treebeard and he replied that he was observing the other guy's fighting techniques while getting pounded and that he was looking forward to partnering the same dude next week. He finished by saying that the best way to learn is by fighting bigger, more experienced fighters.

This guy's utter glee at being able to join in and his totally fearless and pragmatic approach to improving his fighting, was the polar opposite of how I felt when attending. What to me was a chore, was to him a fun time and an opportunity to learn.

It's possible to enjoy anything.

You just have to want to.

------------------------------------------------

*\*\*\* Usually disappointing as they invariably don't remember anything they did.*

*\*\*\*\* Apparently this annual treat was as excruciating to watch as I later imagined, according to both my parents years later.*

47

***** *Countdown to zero where the bomb under the 24 pedestals are deactivated and everyone then has to fight to the death.*

# The Tunnel of Fun

Friday 7th February 2014

After the main session of Krav Maga on a Thursday evening there's that threshold moment. Just after we line up and the instructor gives a quick recap of the evening's training, and then asks the ONE fateful question:

"Who's staying for combat?"

Combat. The bigger brother of the previous 90 minutes. The Merle to Daryl Dixon. The "Let The Right One In" to Twilight. The Battle Royale to The Hunger Games.

Full on fight club. Helmets, gum shields, shin guards, chest guards and boxing gloves. Kicking, punching and going hammer and tongs on each other.

Last night various excuses whirled around in my head. I'd hurt my neck a bit when forward roll training (P4 beckons) and was contemplating using that as an excuse to cry off. Then I thought about the fact that I was already tired when I arrived and that I do a physically tiring job AND it's currently winter in England (Julius Caesar reportedly hated being stationed here as a Centurion before he rose up the ranks of Roman politics…solely due to our lousy weather).

But I put my hand up with everyone else.

A five minute break is etiquette, enabling water bottles

to be refilled and a banana to be scoffed if that's your quick fix of energy. It was a busy session last night and as I looked around the guys getting kitted up, I realised that the "bloke who used to be a boxer" was there.

Also the "bloke who's 6 feet 11 inches and a P5" was there.

Not only that but the "bloke who's built like a brick shithouse and also a P5" was there. My heart began to race a bit, and I was glad I'd taken a beta blocker before I set off** for class.

We partnered up and at the beginning it was just 1 minute fights, constantly changing partners. This was good as it meant we got to see other people's fighting styles and it was pot luck who you got as "choose someone else" was shouted every time the 60 seconds alarm went off.

We move on and practiced some techniques and I was quite enjoying myself.

But then came the big one.

The instructor said "Right, groups of 6" and we stood on opposite sides of the sports hall, waiting to see what he had planned.

Grinning broadly he explained that this was the "tunnel of fun" and number one had to fight no. 2 for 30 seconds.

Then he had to fight numbers 3 and 4 AT THE SAME

TIME for 30 seconds. Then evade knife attacks from number 5…for 30 seconds. Finally try and touch the far wall while number 6 did all he could to stop that from happening…for…you get the idea.

So, as I was number 2 I got to be the scrapper. Problem was that everyone was refreshed and radiant and my first partner was the 6'11" P5 dude. Off we went. I managed to get a couple of kicks and punches in but he caught me a right smacker in the side of my head and has a kick like a (very tall) mule.

Then he made his way down the tunnel of fun until number 3 had a go.

This guy was the ex boxer and it was hard work. I looked over to the other group to see their number 6 pick his opponent up and dangle him upside down.

Christ! That's some strength.

Then 4, 5 and 6 came up to me for a scrap. When it came to my turn to run the tunnel, I sucked up my fear and found a secret stash of adrenalin. I was so tired but determined to give it a good go. Didn't do so badly until I got to number 6 and it was the very tall guy. Thinking he'd be top heavy I aimed for his crotch area with my head and tried to push him over.

He went down, but deliberately so he could pin me like a very aggressive venus fly trap. Arms and legs clamped around me and I could feel the chest guard trying to kiss my lungs.

Finally we stood up and the instructor complimented all of us on how much effort we'd put in and said he was very pleased. My t-shirt was piss-wet through but I felt proud of having stayed to do the class and not backing down.

After we did "Kida!" and had the round of applause, I asked the instructor if he'd heard the expression "The spirit is willing but the flesh is weak".

He replied, "Not for you guys. You guys keep on going."

--------------------------------

*\*\* Only 10mg. Think Chamomile tea's bigger brother.*

# The Stonemason's Hammer

15th February 2014

The next round of Practitioner level gradings is looming ever closer, like a dentist's check up or an optician's appointment. At my Krav class now, we are doing "normal" training for about an hour then splitting off into groups relevant to experience and level.

The P0's (or those who don't want to/ aren't eligible to take a grading) go in one big corner, while the rest of us make our way up the badminton hall in groups of ever decreasing size.

The lads going for G1 make up one corner, although their grading isn't until later in the year unless they want to go up to Scotland.

This is still, for me, a mythical level of utter badassery and mysticism. I had to look at the curriculum before I realised it DOESN'T involve powers of levitation and the ability to breathe fire over an opponent. Maybe that's at E level.

As me and two other guys started working on our P4 techniques, one thing became clear to me very quickly.

I am, at the moment, a rough block of stone and need a stonemason's hammer and chisel to chip away at the block in order to make something recognisable as a level 4

Practitioner.

The techniques at this level are much harder than the previous ones (sounds obvious but the curve is fairly big) and mastering them is taking a bit of practice. The wonderful thing about this though, is that when you get the technique right it makes you feel that you've achieved something special.

While initially perturbed by the difficulty factor it is now a reassuring facet of the P4 prospectus for me, as it means I am fully aware of the responsibility and accountability that come with the higher grades.

Escaping from bear hugs.

Stick attack defences

Scissor kicks.

Sound ominous when written down, but working through them slowly but surely with a good instructor (and the help of my P3/ 4 fellow trainees) the chisel began to fall on the block of stone and slowly a form began to emerge.

It's going to be a few weeks before the work is completed, with a lot of stone chippings on the floor but I know the effort will be worth it.

# Unique Practitioners- Viesturs Vavere

19th February 2014

*Practitioner level 2 student Viesturs Vavere is a Christian priest, originally from Latvia. He trains with Krav Maga Midlands and has been a member since 2012. He has some very interesting views on both Krav and its compatibility with his chosen faith.*

**So, who are you?**

I am Viesturs Vavere from the capital of Latvia, Riga. I was born and bred in Riga. I was born on March 4th 1958.

Riga is a very interesting situation. It's like a country in itself. Most of the population is located in Riga. There is a saying that "if you have been in Riga, you have not been in Latvia". Latvia is a very small, tiny country. The population is about 2 million. You compare this with cities like Birmingham where there are 8 million people, or London where there are 10 million. In the last few years most people have emigrated to other countries like Germany and also the United Kingdom.

**How long have you been a priest?**

I was ordained in 1990, nearly 24 years ago.

**What made you decide to become a priest?**

I was born and bred in the Soviet Union and at that

time people were brainwashed. I was looking for peace of mind so at that time I found it in the church. I decided also that it would be very good for me to become a priest and to preach, so that's the reason.

**Why did you choose the Lutheran faith?**

My parents belonged to this church and so did I. The second reason is that Lutherans don't have to obey this rule of being celibate.

I have a wife and a daughter. The most important thing however, I'm a Christian. We are Christians.

**Why England?**

I was invited by British citizens of Latvian origin who were residing here since 1947. The previous priest had retired and I was invited to take care of the Latvian congregation in the Midlands.

**How many churches do you control?**

I conduct services in 7 venues, in Birmingham, Leicester, Nottingham, Peterborough, Derby...plus Catthorpe and Walston. My flock are about 500 people, not many.

**What attracted you to become a Krav Maga practitioner?**

We live in an increasingly dangerous world and there is a saying "have another day by being safe today."
Also a Christian must be able to protect not only his family but also other people who need help. Be ready for things

that could happen.

**You don't find it strange to be both a priest and a practitioner?**

No. First of all a Christian is a warrior. He is not a bed-wetting wimp. A Christian must know how to fight and how to protect people. You don't take what is written in the Bible literally. If you read very carefully the Old Testament, you can see all these prophets and also judges, like King David and also Samson, they were warriors. There is no contradiction.

**Do your flock know that you practice Krav Maga?**

Yes. They know. They are used to this, they have accepted it. The Bible says our body is a temple of the holy spirit and we must keep it fit. This is very important. God is expecting this from us.

**Have you ever had to use what you've learned in Krav Maga to defend yourself outside the lessons?**

No, not yet.

**Do you think it would be useful if something happened? To protect your loved ones.**

Yes, absolutely yes.

**Who or what inspires you in this world?**

My family and good people and good books. I would say also Krav Maga. Also history. I am going round the country studying the history of England when I have free time.

I find the history of this country fascinating.

**Would you like to get to E5 in Krav Maga?**

Yes, I will try. It depends on whether I am able to perform all these drills and depends on my physical health.

**Eyal Yanilov is in his late 50s and he's Expert level 8/ Master level 3, so I think you'll be OK.**

(Laughs) Yes, I hope so.

**Final question. What would be your motto for life.**

Don't do unto others what doesn't have to be done unto you.

# The Third Option

24th February 2014

Today on Facebook I saw a comment made by Anna Surowiec, a Krav instructor in the UK that said:

*"It's only when you see a mosquito landing on your testicles that you realise that there is always a way to solve problems without using violence".*

Before I started Krav Maga I was, like many people, approaching confrontation and the threat of it with a certain…stubbornness.

For example. I'd see a group of guys walking down the street and they'd be blocking the pavement so others had to either stop or step into the road. I would usually just walk straight through the middle of them. \*\*

Similarly if I saw some drunk guy being a dick in a pub, I'd make a point of staying exactly where I was and not leaving or making any attempt to remove myself from the scene but neither would I look at him unless he tried to speak to me or "start".

Finally I'd always try and help my mates out if things went bad. Problem was this was usually if we'd all had a skinful and while on holiday in Crete (where my father retired to) I've got drunk and had about 5 fights in 6 years and lost most of them.

Reason? Stubbornness and loads of tequila shots and beer don't really make for a nimble footed, hard hitting bar brawler.

The basic backbone of my problem was that I was too obstinate to react with anything other than bravado and anger. Reason? I was afraid of being perceived as cowardly. Looking back on a lot of things that I got involved in (I also used to be both a Special Constable and later a paid police officer) it was a lot of luck that guided me through without getting a kicking or worse.

The overlapping effects on my life of the last 2 years with Krav Maga Midlands are that I can now assess a situation without having to prove that I'm blessed with a heroic heart.

My instructors have always said that the best way to defuse or de-escalate a situation is to simply disengage from it. During knife attack training about 18 months ago, Bartosz asked the group, "If someone comes at you with a knife what should you do?"

We hummed and haahed about a suitable answer for a few seconds but he then said, "Run. If you can, just run. You can't win against a knife. But if you can't run…well, this may help you."

The principles of Krav for me are that it doesn't make you a warrior of the bus station/ pub car park/ dark alley. It does instead give you techniques and skills that help you to survive. At the end of the day the whole thing is geared around survival, not on winning fights.

4 years ago in Crete a guy was robbed at gun point at 3am by a Greek bloke holding a small rifle. I was incensed when I heard this story and talked about wanting to take the gun off him and stick it up his arse. My girlfriend of that time said matter-of-factly, "If you do that and I'm with you and you survive the attempt, you will be single the next morning."

Disengage and if you can't disengage, kick to the bollocks or hit to the throat or (as Bartosz so eloquently put it) be a "nightmare" for your attacker so they fear you and back off and that then allows you to disengage.

Now… instead of being stubborn and getting into situations just to prove I had courage, I'm able to assess a situation and not get involved unless I feel it is necessary.

That doesn't mean that there isn't a part of me that WANTS to fight and stand my ground and stick up for myself and tell the bullies to go to Hell but…now I can be a little wiser re: simply walking the other way or avoiding a situation that could get ugly.

There is always a 3rd option.

-------------------------------------------

*\*\* Have to admit I still do this one. Especially if it's outside the McDonalds on the Parade in Leamington Spa between about 11am and 6pm. Go there, you'll see what I mean.*

# Unique Practitioners- Russell Brotherston

25th February 2014

*Russell Brotherston is one of the instructors at Krav Maga Midlands UK and also runs Junior Safe Krav Maga, a kids Krav club.*

**So, who are you?**
I'm Russell Brotherston, I'm 34 years old and I'm a G4 level Krav Maga Midlands instructor and have been for the last two years. I also live in Stratford-upon-Avon.

**What did you do before you became a Krav Maga instructor?**

I did a few things. I worked for a charity for about 11 years. Mainly working around nursing homes doing recovery. It wasn't elderly it was anyone who was 18 to 65. Specialising mainly in schizophrenia, bi-polar, manic depressive…that sort of thing. So there was a lot of unpredictable behaviour. Also did community support for the same charity in and around Coventry. That was going to visit adults but also keeping my eyes peeled for if I thought there was any child abuse going on. Levels of assessment involved there. I also did some work on the acute wards in hospitals.

**What does that involve?**

The acute wards are mainly centred around people who are going on or coming off medication so their behaviour is very unpredictable. Sometimes people who have mental health problems but they haven't been assessed yet. So for example people who've been arrested who are dangerous and they don't know where to put them so they put them on an acute ward.

**What attracted you to Krav Maga as a practitioner in the first place?**

Well, I'd done lots of martial arts before. I'd done Judo, Muay-Thai, Kickboxing and European Kickboxing. I also do some normal boxing as well. All of those seemed very rule orientated. There wasn't really any room for changing. The thing I liked about Krav was that it was the first thing I'd seen where you could spar with like 3 or 4 guys at the same time. You don't do that in any other fighting sport. The most I've heard is in Jiu Jitsu going against two people. I also liked the fact that there was no specific rules so there's room to develop your own style. Not everyone has the same strengths and weaknesses. I'd see videos on the internet and there'd be people doing different defences for the exact same problem.

I was thinking "are these different schools?" but then you'd see them on the exact same promotional video for the exact same club. So they were allowing them flexibility.

And of course, the one that everyone likes. You get to do groin strikes.

**Did you feel you needed to learn Krav for your job?**

Yeah, because when I was working in the mental health sector they don't want you to do any proper self defence which is quite strange.

**Did they give you any self defence training?**

We did breakaway training which is done learning very dated techniques. The instructor told me he'd been teaching the exact same thing for 30 years. He hadn't got any qualifications in self defence. He had one for doing Jiu Jitsu. But he didn't talk that much about "what if there's a problem?"

For example he was talking about someone choking you from the front and he showed us a solution that that WOULD work…provided the attacker attacked you in a very specific way. He didn't make that clear or anything so when he got me to choke him and I held him in a way that wasn't good for the technique he was like, "No, no. Put your arms like this!"

But I didn't get any breakaway training until about six years into the job when me and another member of staff were assaulted by patients on the same day, but at different centres. That's what prompted it. Came out of nowhere. That's what happens in the mental health world. I had to react in a calm way which the job hadn't prepared me for. They'd prepared me more in the hospital but only marginally.

**Do you feel the training they gave you was for insurance and health and safety compliance rather than keeping you safe?**

Yeah, completely. I'd been there 11 years and I did one breakaway training course for one day, that with the lunch break probably lasted about six hours, half of which was the instructor talking. A Q&A session about how people get stressed and you can calm them down by talking. We probably did about two and a half hours of physical work and I never broke a sweat the whole time. It was rubbish to be honest.

I saw the advert for Krav Maga Midlands when I had to take someone to the police station, the flyer was up in the reception. That was about two years before I became an instructor. I went to loads of lessons, asked Bartosz for lots of tips and had my punchbag in my garage where I practiced for about 6 days a week for at least an hour, hour and a half, just going through strikes.

**Did your hospital or the other organisations tell you not to use self defence tactics but only to disengage from a violent situation?**

Yeah, that's basically what you're meant to do. That's what breakaway training is.

It only works for if someone goes to grab you. It's not for if someone tries to punch you or kick you or stab you. There was one incident I heard of where a patient grabbed a fire extinguisher and chased someone down the corridor. The real element that happens is that people at work do what they need to do to get out of a situation. I know a woman attacked by 5 or 6 patients at the same time in the canteen. All she could do was hide under the table. Legally we're not meant to go in and do anything, but another guy ran in, grabbed her arms and dragged her out. He was legally meant to leave her to be beaten up, that's what they say you should do. Which I find disgusting. That's one of the reasons I got out of it as I thought there was no way I was getting sued for defending myself.

When the guy punched me they asked me if I wanted to press charges. Friends were saying I should as he knew it was wrong. But from the standpoint of the company it's just a hazard of the job.

**On a more cheerful note. You teach kids as young as 6 Krav Maga?**

The stuff I teach the kids in class is different. Kids don't have that fear element. You know with forward rolls you build up to it in height. Kids will ask me to put the pad for them to jump over at about chest height. They take to it because the only similar thing is something like Tae Kwon Do where you stand in a formal line, it's very uniformed and you're put in with the adults.

Kids don't like to learn like that. They like to run around and play so you put it in the format of a game. For them it's playing, building their co-ordination and motor skills. Their parents watching from the side can see the self defence connotations.

**It's interesting with the hospitals and charities not wanting you go hands on, the irony is that children, with all those rules around contact and DBS clearance to work with them and we're teaching the next generation a much more common sense approach including kicking to the groin.**

Exactly. I talk to the parents first so they know that it's Krav, it's a physical thing. I'm going to be playing rough and tumble games with their kids picking their kids up, spinning them round. I'm going to be wrestling like 3 or 4 at once, they're going to be trying to pin me down (laughs). It's just part of the thing. You've got to teach them that if they're not running away or making a lot of noise. A bunch of 6 or 7 kids can quite happily take out an adult if they're punching and kicking. That's what they do to me. They don't get the chance to do that anywhere else. The stuff they learn with me is specifically for class or if something serious happens. The hard thing is convincing them not to try the tactics on other kids.

In the kids' classes they learn two responses to everything. Response against a child and another to an adult. If a kid grabs them in a bear hug then they can't really start kicking them in the groin or elbowing them in the head. They do Rapping On The Barn Door which is rapping the knuckles so they person lets go which won't work on an adult.

**Which do you prefer teaching? Adults or children?**

(Laughs) It's a totally different thing. Well I can teach adults for a lot longer. Children's classes are tiring. It's 6 of 1 and half a dozen of the other. Kids when they're in great mood can be so much fun, they really can engage. At the same time they can get really wound up and get really hyper and get quite disobedient. So it's a question of keeping their attention so you stop and start, stop and start. Ideally I'd like a child's energy in an adult. Kids can go on for games for ages. Adult games like 1 or 2 minutes, with kids it's about 5. They run and run until you tell them to stop.

**Any advice to anyone wanting to become a Krav Maga instructor?**

Do like I did. Train and train and train. Anything like sports, the basic things you know just keep doing them, fast and slow again and again. A good idea is to get a camera and film yourself so you can see what you're doing.

Another is to get together with students you know, preferably of a higher level so you're always training with people with more knowledge than you. Like when I did basketball I played with better people. Eventually I could compete with them but for a long time they thrashed me (laughs).

**What would be your motto for life?**

Do not be too timid or squeamish about your actions. All life is an experiment. The more experiments you make, the better.

## Fully Cocked

9th March 2014

As the next grading looms ever nearer, like Megatron over the horizon, I find myself unsure of whether to actually grade or not.

I always vowed I'd never go in for one unless I believed I was 100% ready. Reason being that if I train to the max, give it my all and THEN flunk the grading I will merely be upset for a day or two and then jump up, dust myself off and retrain.

However....

At my P3 grading last year both Jon Bullock (Head of KMG UK) and Rune Lind (E4 Examiner) said before we started, "From this point forward it is not about collecting patches. Here's where it gets harder." \*\*

As much as I want that extra bar on the patch on the left leg of my KMM training pants. As much as I know I will feel like solid gold when I pass. As much as I KNOW just how proud I will be...I also know that to go in half cocked is a bad idea.

Some people say, "Treat the grading as a day out and a chance to assess what you've learned. Pass or fail it's a stepping stone."

While that may be true, I'm only human and will feel

like crap if I fail the grading as that's what human beings do. So...I've decided that if I'm not ready I'm not going to go for it.

How to make sure one way or the other?

Well...

I'm in the wonderful position of belonging to a club that has 6 separate venues and 3 instructors, Monday to Friday.

There's also a pre grading workshop the week before the actual test that I'll be attending.

And just maybe I'll arrange a session of private tuition with one of my instructors to iron out the creases.

There is no shame in failing if you've given it your all. Only if you go in half cocked.

*\*\* And Jesus Christ did it!!! My T-shirt resembled a dishcloth after.*

## The Jigsaw

18th March 2014

As the pieces come together with regard to my training for P4...it's the little things that seem to make a difference. I'm more nervous now than I have been for any of the other gradings and was having severe palpitations over Scissor Kicks and Forward> Backward Rolls.

Finally getting the roll right was a Moment. As was finally managing to kick with the same foot I'd just launched myself off the floor with.

I invested in a mirror last week. Only £10 from Argos and it's a big one that I can prop up against the wall in my bedroom and then practice the moves from the P4 DVD. This has proved invaluable as, with the laptop next to me on the bed, I can copy and repeat the moves until I've got them nailed.

The club I belong to, Krav Maga Midlands, have classes Monday to Friday in one of 6 venues around the area. Last week I went 4 times, this week it's 3 (St Patrick's day intervened) and next week will be 4 again.

We also have a pre-grading workshop on Sunday 23rd March in Stratford-upon-Avon and I might just invest in a private lesson with one of the instructors to really add some shine to the polish.

Overall this is feeling like a huge jigsaw. At the start it was just a mess of shapes, but now I can see the picture emerging as the pieces come together.

## The Dress Rehearsal

23rd March 2014

Like most people I get a little nervous before important events in life.

Job interviews; a date with a pretty lady; phoning up to find out why NPower have increased my direct debit by £86 and never told me.**

For the last 2 or 3 weeks I've felt nervous about my upcoming grading for Practitioner level 4.

I've talked about private lessons with one of the instructors. I've been attending KMM sessions 3 or 4 times per week at different venues. I've rationalised with an abacus and a slide rule and a magic ball that "mixing it up" is a good idea so I deliberately go to venues with different instructors (we have 3). I have been practicing in front of a mirror in my bedroom with my laptop on the bed, while Zeev Cohen and Eyal Yanilov demonstrate the moves for P4 on the official DVD.

Today we had the Pre-Grading Workshop in Stratford-upon-Avon. This was planned as an opportunity to "iron out" any wrinkles in our skill sets and set us up for next week.

Two of our three instructors oversaw this and to my immense delight it turned out to be just what I needed.

We split into various groups, according to grade, on the mats and got to work with the various moves and techniques that would have to be demonstrated at an actual grading. Behind a curtain in the other side of the sports hall were about 200 kids and their parents. A Tae Kwon Do (sp?) tournament for little 'uns was going on and a few of them came over for a look.

One parent seemed overly unimpressed, simply watching us work out with a poker face the entire time. However two little boys thought the stick disarms that me and the other P4 candidates were performing were "well cool."

I also got distracted during choke releases by the endearing and unbelievably cute (but hysterical) sight of a 7 year old in a kimono, helmet and boxing gloves SKIPPING past us with her mother.

Working through our techniques built a LOT of reassurance into the training. I'd seriously been thinking of canning my grading till October if I wasn't ready the week before but as the training wore on, I felt more and more self-assured and I know my training buddy Graham felt the same way.

Biggest arse ache for me in the last few weeks was Scissor Kick. Designed for when you want to run at and kick someone who is running at you, it means leaping off the floor and then kicking with the same foot you launched with. Finally cracked this one today which, along with the Stick Disarms, really boosted my confidence.

The forward rolls for this level include doing a combo of Forward> Backward but without getting up or stopping (i.e. roll, twist, roll again). I had this nailed when we were confronted by two separate piles of strike pads and told to roll over them. The first was high, the second was long. After a few fumbles and knocking the first pile over a couple of times I got it.

At the end the groups had combat scenarios appropriate to their level with Ps 1 and 2 doing ground-based fighting (i.e. wrestling) and us plus P3 having the delightful joys of "3 against 1" for a minute each as a stand up fight with 16 oz boxing gloves or MMA mitts on.

After it was all over I personally felt 70% more in charge of my destiny than I had before we started. Revision is the key in gradings and this crash course had done its work for me and the others.

A great day of prep, and also great to see members from the other classes that KMM runs (Solihull, Coventry, Birmingham, Banbury, Rugby and Leamington Spa as well as Stratford-upon-Avon).

Counting down to the grading with relish now.

## P4 Grading: P Flawed
## London Copperbox Arena, Olympic Park.

29th March 2014

I had what could politely be described as an "anxious" week in the build up to my latest grading. Bitten nails, lack of sleep, fear of failure and just to rub salt in it...a cold four days beforehand meaning I would wake up at 4am coughing, with my face resembling a half melted candle.

Practitioner 3 had been initiation into the "Big Boys Club".

P4 was fighting for the right to remain there.

I was in two minds up until the Dress Rehearsal that KMM ran last week, as to whether I should postpone my grading until October. I had no fear of humiliation if I was to fail after going in fully prepped. However I did not wish to go in half cocked and crash out just because of wanting the extra bar on my patch.

After the confidence boost from the pre-grading workshop the demons of despair decided to give me a mild dose of the common cold. As working out or exercising while ill is a minefield at the best of times, I planned a strategy of only going to two classes in the run up to the grading AND not going at all on the day preceding it.

This turned out to be a good idea as my body had time to recover and my mind was more or less clear of Kravvy thoughts on the Friday.

One of the big scares in the build up was knowing that the chief examiner on the day would be Zeev Cohen. Master level 1/ Expert level 6.

One of my club's instructors had passed his Kids Instructor's course with Zeev as a tutor and said how good but also how focused on perfecting the techniques Zeev is.

So...a face full of phlegm, not 100% confident on passing and the number 2 for Krav Maga Global would be there on the day. To put it mildly...I was bit nervous.

Due to problems with the Birmingham venue at the October 2013 grading, KMG UK had decided to hold only three in England this time. One in London, one in Bristol and one in Penrith. I chose London but most of KMM seemed destined for Bristol. Luckily two guys were heading down for P4 as well and we pooled a car to head down.

Morning of the grading finally came to dawning with all the speed of continental drift. I had to drive for an hour to where my mate lives to share the ride but my Sat Nav decided to throw a tantrum about 10 miles from his house. Instead of simply flashing up "Location Unknown" it kept taking me to obscure villages and three left turns in a row (i.e. a circle).

I finally rocked up about 45 minutes later swearing my head off and the three of us piled in his 4x4 and headed off to London.

When we got the venue we had over an hour to spare. The Copperbox Arena is a hangover from the last Olympics and a well designed and vast complex. We headed up to watch the P1 and P2 guys going through their paces in the final stages of their grading. To see such a vast amount of people in one place ALL being tested took my breath away. There had been about 50 Practitioners at my P1 grading in October 2012 but here there were 100+, all going through the motions while 6 examiners walked around with white polo shirts and clipboards marking down scores. Zeev himself was blending in well, with a blue jacket on, and not standing out at all. As he was roaming around the hall checking people out and watching ground releases, it made it clear that he was taking this seriously as was everyone else.

When things finally wrapped up for P1 and P2 they separated into two groups and awaited their fate.

We were told that individual feedback was to be given this time along with your percentage score.

Our registration opened and we queued up to be handed a number that need to be pinned to the back of our t-shirts and an endearing "Yanilov dollar" that allowed us £5 off any KMG merchandise purchased that day from the store at the side of the room.

As the clock ticked ever nearer to our proposed start time we assembled on the other side of the curtain dividing the hall and went through a few stretches and techniques. Everyone was looking nervous and we could hear rounds of applause and names being called out as our predecessors collected their patches and certificates. I got chatting to two guys from a London club and one was showing me some last minute wrist grab releases.

A few endearing urban myths about Zeev were doing the rounds while we waited. One was that he'd once walked into a P4 grading and failed everybody in the room after 10 minutes with only the words "Not aggressive enough!" before walking out again. My emotions were clearly showing on my face when one guy looked at me and smiled, saying "Don't worry about it, it's all just bullshit."

We started about an hour later than we thought we would but as there were

(thankfully) no clocks on the walls, we didn't really mind beyond wanting the stomach butterflies to get lost.

We were told to form four lines, with pairs facing each other making two tunnels of partners. I was without a grading buddy as my two mates had partnered each other. After yelling "Anyone need a partner?" I got introduced to a really friendly French guy named Ian who was 56 and a former boxer.

Said he'd been doing Krav for about 5 years but had been slow on taking the gradings.

Once we had our places marked out we were told to remember where we were standing and Jon Bullock called us over with a microphone (room was THAT big, he needed one). There appeared to be about 150 of us, most going for P4. He asked us to shout out how we felt right now. Answers ranged from "positive" and "determined" to "nervous" and "scared". Jon pointed out that the answers were both negative and positive and then said:

"Turn to the person next to you and you have 30 seconds to tell them EXACTLY how you feel right now, then it's their turn. GO!"

Ian was nearest to me so I blurted out my fears and phobias and anxiety while he smiled and nodded reassuringly. Then he told me that he wanted to pass but it was not the end of the world for him but he was a little nervous.

Jon then pointed out that our faces looked a little different now. His next tool to boost our positive energy was to tell us: "Now tell the person nearest to you what passing this grading will mean to you. GO!"

Same again and by the time we'd finished some people were even laughing. Jon said that this had changed the mood and added that success is 80% motivation and 20%

physical. He then added the finishing touch which was that we were to stand up and assure our partners that they WOULD pass and we knew and believed in them.

Cue a lot of smiling and hugging and claps on the back. Feeling a lot more confident and relaxed I took my place opposite Ian and finally we kicked off.

Due to the sheer amount of people (50 or so in P4 and the rest spread between 3 and 5) we had to wait a while before we had an examiner walk up to assess us. We were told to practice the moves relevant to the level at about 50 to 60% and only to go "hammer and tongs" if the examiner was with us.

Me and Ian were the second to last pair on our row and when we got to choke hold releases the examiner made Ian grab me again, saying "Don't try to be a friend. Grab him properly now!" We did the moves and then moved on to stick and knife attacks plus bears hugs while constantly refreshing techniques and keeping a crafty eye open for what was going on just down the row, as our examiner moved closer and was asking people to show specific movements and releases.

When our technical abilities were finally done and dusted, we got called into a huddle and told to put on shin guards, forearm guards, gum shields and MMA gloves.

We were all tired by this point, which the examiners

blatantly knew and one said, "Here's where you have to suck it all up." We were told to fight for 2 minutes with hands only, then 2 with feet only, then 2 with hands and feet, then finally 2 with a stick or knife nearby to attack our opponent with. Each round had to be a new partner.

I knew from the milling we'd had on P3 that this would be hard but I'd forgotten just how exhausting this type of thing can be. My first two rounds weren't so bad and by the time we got to "hands and feet" I'd chosen a partner who knew how to box so he caught me a few meaty smackers in the jaw.

By the time we got to the final session I was with a guy who grappled with me and I lost my left contact lens. He was a gent and paused when I told him, but I realised I wouldn't be able to find it let alone put it back in so just carried on. Same dude then dislodged my gum shield which I decided not to retrieve either. Big mistake as his next punch chipped one of my front teeth. I finally managed to clinch with him and punched him up close a few times before the much appreciated "STOP!" was shouted across the hall.

Guessing we were far from finished I wasn't surprised when we were told to put on 16oz full boxing gloves and go again. The examiner said: "We have about fifteen minutes left, we hope to get as many rounds in as we can. Two minutes again, change partners each time but feel free to try and take your partner to the floor. Punch him a little bit, then get up and fight again."

We were now resembling combat-ready versions of The Walking Dead and as we began to fight you could hear the panting and groaning. While I was fighting I tried a tackle but realised that unless my opponent was as tired as me and not much stronger, then chances are I wouldn't get him down. Then the opportunity arose when I saw two people come tumbling down behind him, which he hadn't noticed. Seizing the moment I shoved him over them both and followed him down. A roving examiner watched us tussle for a few seconds then yelled, "GET UP AGAIN! FIGHT!" GET UP!"

As we changed partners again I could feel my arms and legs getting heavier. I knew we were being judged on aggression and resilience and was determined not to give in. While scrapping this time a guy wandered up and began punching me, despite the fact that I already had a partner.

I had enough mental function left to realise he was the "odd number" from when we'd started and had been told to roam around and randomly pick on existing pairs.

The examiner finally stopped the fighting and had another surprise for us. We now had to fight for 2 minutes BUT it was to be groups of 3 with 2 against 1.

I felt a gentle tug on my arm and it was my buddy

from KMM, who jerked his head to indicate I should join them. As we kicked off it was simply a case of fighting through the fatigue and remembering not to get cornered or "go between them." When the fighting was finally over we had one final surprise waiting for us.

"OK everyone. To finish: 60 push ups; 60 crunches; 60 squats and 60 burpies."

The groaning was audible and one brave soul panted, "16?"

The examiner grinned and went, "Nice try, no. SIXTY!"

I managed all the push ups, crunches and squats, but lost the ability to remember my own name by the time I got to the burpies (think I probably maxed out at about 40 before I fell face down on the floor).

We then stumbled over to get water and peel off our sodden protective gear while we recovered, wolfed down a banana or a granola bar, and waited to hear our fate.

P3 and P5 got their results first as they were smaller groups and after about an hour the examiners apologised for keeping us waiting and invited us to sit on the floor around them to hear our scores.

There was much grunting and creaking of joints as sore bodies were lowered to the gymnasium floor.

They made it clear that there were three results. A pass, a technical pass and a fail. A technical pass meant that while you had achieved the minimum grade of 70% or

more, you were lacking in one or more things that they
that they felt you should improve on to satisfaction, before you would be awarded your certificate. Bottom line was that you had passed BUT your own club's instructors would have to sign you off as competent in the grey areas and THEN give you your patch.

As the numbers were read out, people raised their hands and the scores were given. A guy behind me was one of the first names called and had achieved 92%. He was beaming, clearly over the moon and the examiners congratulated him on having the highest score. One of my mates was called next and had a high score of 82%. I though he was through and clear when the examiner then added that he needed to be reassessed on bear hugs.

Before long someone was told they "need to retest". On previous, smaller gradings this was done privately
beforehand, with people being taken to one side and informed they had failed. This time the information was given flatly and the examiner then moved on.
It was bad seeing the hurt and disappointment on people's faces and as my name hadn't been read out yet I could feel my nerves jangling once more.

My partner Ian had the second highest score of 91% and was congratulated personally. My number was next and I was optimistic of a similar score until the examiner said "73%, you need to retake stick defences."

I nodded my acknowledgment and was monumentally relieved to have passed while still narked off to have to wait before I could get the sewing kit out once I got home.

There were so many people who had to retake stick defences that the examiner eventually started saying something like "Number 253? 78%. Sticks" and then moving on without elaborating. Of the 50 or so people at around me, roughly 20 passed outright, 20 passed but had to be reassessed on one area back at their club and 10 or 11 failed.

This was the hardest grading I'd been to where the expectations were set at a very high level.

Finally we applauded as the guys went up to collect their patches and certificates and then made our way out. It was only then that I noticed Zeev Cohen again who was chatting with Jon Bullock near the doors. He'd taken personal charge of overseeing the P5 gradings and hadn't taken part in our assessments. As I looked back into the vast hall, the edges were littered with empty mineral water bottles, chocolate bar wrappers and the odd banana skin.

I rang Al one of our club's instructors to tell him we'd passed and asked if we could do the reassessments the following Monday in two days. He laughed and said not but reassured me not to worry and congratulated us all on getting through.

We piled into the nearest service station on the M40 for something to eat and I can't remember the last time I've finished two bags of fries, a double chicken 'n' bacon burger, a big piece of fried chicken, a pot of baked beans and a litre of Tango before (with ice cream for pud).

This was an emotionally and physically draining experience. A week with little sleep, training with a cold, fingernails bitten till they bled. Stress. Anxiety. Lost contact lens. Lost gum shield. Chipped tooth. Exhaustion. Bruising AND a resit of stick defences to come.

It was worth it.

Bring on P5.

## Unique Practitioners- Lewis Turpin

### 2nd April 2014

*Randolph Adolphus Turpin was born in Leamington Spa in 1928 and grew up in the neighbouring town of Warwick. He became the World Middleweight Boxing champion in 1951 when he defeated Sugar Ray Robinson. He is considered by many to be the best middleweight boxer of the 1940s and 1950s. He was inducted into the International Boxing Hall of Fame in 2001.*

*A bronze statue of him was unveiled by Sir Henry Cooper in the Market Square in the centre of Warwick in 2001.*

*Randolph's grand nephew Lewis Turpin is now a Krav Maga practitioner with Krav Maga Midlands.*

**So, introduce yourself.**

I'm Lewis Turpin, 29, from Leamington Spa. I've been doing Krav since October so about 6 months now. Took a grading recently, smashed the P1. All good.

**What do you know about your uncle Randolph?**

One of the best pound for pound fighters of his time. He was one of three brothers. There was Randolph, Jackie and Dick. Dick was my granddad. He was the eldest of the three and actually taught Randy boxing to start off with. Their father, Fitzbert was the first black person to live in Warwick.

He died when they were all quite young so they had to look after themselves. They used to do bare knuckle fighting up Warwick market when the gypsies used to come to town My granddad challenged the black barrier for England so that coloured people could fight in championship bouts. He was the British & Commonwealth champion.

He was the first black person to win a British boxing title but Randy went all the way. He was the one that won the world championship.

**Was your father, Dick's son, a boxer too?**

I think he dabbled, he did a bit. I know he stopped boxing when mum was pregnant with me. He stopped and then that was it. Apparently he was pretty good.

**Did he ever take a title?**

No, he didn't climb that high. None of the family has really bothered with it, that sort of thing. I mean I wish I'd done something when I was younger. I used to go boxing when I was 8 or 9. I used to really enjoy it. Used to go on the weekends but I got a bit bored in the end. I wasn't doing anything, wasn't going anywhere. They said "you have to be 12 or 13 to fight." My mind just slipped. You get bored when you're a kid, just doing the same things over and over again. I just lost interest really. Uncle Jackie had a gym and I was training there.

**What do you remember of your granddad and uncles?**

I never met Randy, he died in like the 60s. I barely remember my granddad Dick. He died when I was quite young. Jackie I obviously knew as he died not so long ago.

**What attracted you to Krav Maga as opposed to carrying on with boxing?**

I won't lie, if I could go back in time I'd do boxing but I've always wanted to do something that involves a bit of everything. I was going to do MMA but then I looked on the Internet and Krav came up. Never even heard of it before. Seen the website and was thinking 'better try this out'. It was only up the road from me. I Googled it to check it all out to see what it was like and I was like 'Wow! This is definitely something I want to do.' Also it's realism based. Being 29, if I wanted to be a boxer, most boxers retire in their early 30s.

Too many punches to the head. No point starting boxing at that age if you know what I mean. I'm so glad I found it to be fair.

**What level would you like to get to in Krav?**

As far as I can go.

**Expert 5?**

Could do yeah. Would be hard for me but I wouldn't mind pushing it as far as I can go. 29 now so still got plenty of time.

**Do any other members of your family, brothers, sisters or cousins do boxing or martial arts?**

No. No one. I'm flying the flag. I wish I had carried the family name. Now I'm doing Krav and some type of contact sport I actually think like, well wish I'd done something years ago instead of going out on the piss. That's pretty much all I ever did when I was younger. It was at the back of my mind 'why don't you do boxing?' but the party lifestyle sort of took over. Never really thought of it. Only when I started hitting nearly 30 I thought 'right, gotta knuckle down and get fit!' Gym was one thing but I've always wanted to do something physical. Since I started Krav I haven't looked back.

**What would your motto for life be?**

It is what it is. Deal with it.

## Pump Room Action
## Krav Maga Midlands- Night Parks Training

Tuesday 8th April 2014

Due to a double booking at Krav Maga Midlands' usual Tuesday training ground in Trinity school, Leamington Spa, Bartosz decided to improvise and take us all out on a little trip to get back to nature.

Royal Leamington Spa has some gorgeous parks and now Spring is finally in the air, the Pump Room gardens next to the town library were utilised for the welcome return of the Night Park Scenarios training that we last attempted in Stratford-upon-Avon in Autumn 2013.

After meeting up near the river bridge we took to the elevated walkway next to York Road at the back of the old library near Station Approach. The whole thing seemed a little surreal with me and the other practitioners warming up while people walking dogs, joggers, and cyclists all made their way past us with confused looks on their faces. Some even took a detour to avoid us.

After some ever-necessary stretching and loosening up we started on 3rd party protection. This was what it says on the tin, where you have to protect your "mate" from a frontal attack by a roving scallywag (or in this case, another practitioner).

One technique which is fundamental in this type of thing, is that you MUST remember to extricate your 3rd Party from the situation as soon as you have neutralised or reduced the attack.

Reason? In real life people try to get involved or are panicking or just plain pissed off to have someone try and take a swing at them.

Ever tried to defend a drunken yet outspoken girlfriend on a night out? My own experiences of witnessing this are that she will at least want to "have words" with the other party. The removal technique was to spin them round, grab their right arm with your right hand and grab their neck with your left (or vice versa) then push them in the direction you want them to go until you are both clear of danger.

The next technique involved if you are holding hands and someone tries to give you trouble, as your defence technique needs to adapt accordingly. Cue much laughter as some of the butchest blokes in the club were required to walk along with fingers entwined as if they were on a moonlit stroll along Brighton beachfront.

Later we moved to choke holds and then knife defences. The latter proved tricky as we were on hard ground but it's always satisfying to get a bigger opponent onto the floor, just by applying the correct leverage to their wrist.

A few times we had members of the public wander through the group including a father with two wide eyed toddlers, several joggers, and a woman leading a dog on a length of old rope. She looked at us in bewilderment for a few seconds and asked, "Is this a fight or are you pretending to fight?" She then added that the dog was a stray she'd found and wondered if any of us would like to take it off her.

We all politely declined.

After the main techniques had been gone through, the daylight had faded and the park lamps had sprung into life. Bartosz then said, "Number yourselves from 1."

I got in first and then the remaining numbers were argued over. Bartosz told me to wait and took the other lads to where the path runs from the bridge, around the back of where we'd been training before it rejoins the trail. After some whispering and muttered instructions he came to fetch me and said grinning, "OK Lance, just walk from one end to the other."

Even though I'd done this before and even though these were all my club mates and EVEN THOUGH it was a training scenario...there is something very creepy about seeing about 12 guys in black clothing, loitering silently around a dark alleyway in staggered formation, grinning and clearly planning mischief.

First guy simply wanted to ask the time, a red herring

I've seen before so I politely declined and moved on. The second tried to grab me and I managed to kick him away before I reached the joys of the middle bit where I got attacked with knives by two guys at once and then jumped by three blokes pretending to mug me. I got through relatively unscathed and was pleased before swapping places with number 2. Each guy went through and Bartosz changed the roles of each "attacker" every time so that no one could predict what they would have to face. Funniest variation was a fairly big lad who was told to grab the person as if he was a drunken mate just wanting a hug. It didn't take long before someone's adrenalin got the better of them and they booted the guy asking the time straight in the groin rather than seeing it as a benign request.

Finally we'd all got through and we regrouped up the top for the final "Kida" and made our way home.

I thoroughly enjoyed tonight's training. Mainly as it worked on techniques that are incredibly useful if out with friends or on a date, but also because moving through the Tunnel of Fun in semi darkness and taking on loads of people is just such F.U.N.

## Hannah and Daddy (A Story)

25th April 2014

*I wrote this last October. It's a fictional story about an infant girl and her father. Idea came after reading about a Krav Maga car jacking seminar which got me thinking.*
*The ending's satisfying.*

Hannah was scared. She'd seen Daddy shouting at the man who'd put his head in their car. She was crying too. In her chair in the back of Daddy's car she wanted to help Daddy but she couldn't as she was strapped in. Daddy had opened the door of the car and the man had been knocked down. The man had a gun like her brother Dominic. This one had made a nasty bang though as the man had been knocked down and Hannah's ears hurt and it had made her jump. Daddy had then got out and he had hit the man many times. Hannah didn't like the man, he'd frightened her and upset her Daddy. She loved Daddy. Her and Daddy had been shopping and Daddy had let her ride on his shoulders and he'd bought her some candy floss and thrown her up in the air and they'd laughed and laughed and Hannah was so happy.

Then they'd got back in the car and Daddy had put her in

her seat and had smiled and ruffled her hair and she was so happy because she'd had such a lovely day with Daddy and then the man had appeared. He smelled horrid and he had hair on his face like Daddy did some mornings but worse and he'd shouted some things and pointed his gun like Dominic's at Daddy and then at Hannah.

Hannah had wanted to shout at the man to go away and leave her and Daddy alone but the man kept shouting. She couldn't see Daddy and the man now, they were shouting though, she could hear them. Daddy was using bad words like he smacked Dominic for saying and some other words that Hannah didn't know. Daddy and the man were shouting. There was another loud bang and Hannah screamed, crying more than before. She struggled in her seat and the straps hurt her arms.

They were in the big car park that Hannah liked as they got to drive up and up and up. She got Daddy to drive them right to the top and she could see for such a long, long way across the big town.

"Daddy!" she screamed, "DADDY!"

Daddy stood up, he was breathing funny and he had blood on his face, on his chin. Hannah screamed in fright and Daddy smiled at her. He was holding the nasty man's gun, like Dominic's.

"Hi baby. It's ok," Daddy said smiling again.

Hannah was so pleased that Daddy was OK. She

couldn't see the man but she heard him say something and Daddy turned around, his face becoming angry and he kicked out. She heard the man shout and then he was quiet. Daddy put his head in the car and smiled at her again.

"Are you okay Daddy?" Hannah said, still crying. She hoped Daddy was OK and the nasty man hadn't hurt him.

"I'm fine baby," Daddy said giving her a kiss and putting the gun on the seat where Mummy sat when they went out with Dominic too.

"Who's that man Daddy?" Hannah asked, her tears drying as she saw Daddy was OK.

"He's just a silly man baby. Listen Hannah, I need you to be a brave girl and do something for me ok?"

Hannah paused, her tears stopping and she nodded, "OK Daddy."

Daddy looked down at where the man was and he looked angry again for a moment, then he turned back to her and smiled. "I need you to close your eyes and sing a song for me ok? Remember that nursery rhyme we sang about Jack Be Nimble? Can you sing that for me now baby? But you must close your eyes!" Hannah nodded and Daddy leaned in again to kiss her forehead. "There's a good girl," he said. "Now please sing it Hannah, close your eyes and don't open them until Daddy says so OK."

Hannah nodded again and closed her eyes tightly. She

began to sing unsteadily," Jack be nimble, jack be quick, jack....jump...err...over the candle stick."

"Brilliant baby. Just keep singing it as loud as you can and keep your eyes closed ok?"

Hannah kept her eyes shut tight and kept singing the song Daddy had sung to her at bedtime a few days ago. While she was singing she could still hear Daddy start shouting at the man again.

## *"THREATEN MY F\*\*\*KING DAUGHTER?!!" YOU F\*\*\*ING C\*\*T!!! YOU'RE FINISHED MATE!!!"*

"No please I'm sorry. NO!"

Hannah heard the man shout again then his voice faded away.

After a few seconds there was a loud crash, like when Dominic had fallen over the dustbins in the back garden.

She opened her eyes and saw Daddy looking over the wall in front of the car, the one that looked out so very high over the big town.

Daddy turned and saw she'd opened her eyes. She thought he'd be cross but he smiled at her again and walked to the car.

He took the gun like Dominic's off the seat, wiped it with his sleeve (why did he do that?) and threw it over the wall. Then he came back to the car. "There's a good girl, bit of silly behaviour from that man eh? Nothing to worry about."

"Where's the man gone Daddy?" Hannah asked looking around, the straps in her seat stopping her from seeing behind her.

Daddy sat in the seat and closed the door. He started the engine of the car and made it go backwards. "He ran away baby. He ran away."

They drove home singing again, Daddy forgot the words a few times but Hannah remembered them all.

## Pick 'n' Mix

29th April 2014

My Krav club have several venues. Through trying them out I've now find a bespoke fitting for my own comfort zone around both training and combat.

Never much liked combat. Love the technical side of Krav but really couldn't get into the swing of taking a swing at someone on a cold blooded basis once a week.

This is simply something I needed to deal with and I've tried several options. Forcing myself to go. Picking the biggest bloke present as a partner. Picking the highest qualified bloke as a partner**. Getting up and coming back when knocked down. And professional help outside of Krav. Really didn't change my view of it all and in fact the state of "not liking it much" simply persisted.

I love Krav Maga as it keeps me fit and the skills are unsurpassable as tools for life in a physically confrontational situation. KMM have 3 instructors spread over 6 venues, Monday to Friday. I've been trying out the various locations for a month or so and have finally hit upon a recipe that works for me.

My grade is P4, but to be honest my fighting ability is pretty low. I lack the skills and while I'll stand my ground I tend very often to get a hefty boot in the groin or drop my guard long enough to get a right hook in the head. At my home club the guys who opt for combat are either long stayers or high grades (we currently have five P5s and they semi-regularly attend this class) or both. The class isn't enjoyable for me solely because I'm not able to keep up.

Some believe that if you fight much better and experienced guys then you improve. This is true, but you need to start somewhere and if, like me, you are simply uncomfortable with it then another solution must be sought.

On Monday I go to one class where there are loads of people who stay for Combat and they are in the majority relatively new. There are a mixture of abilities so I can relax a little and work on my footwork, dodging and strikes. I stayed last night and thoroughly enjoyed the class, and was partnered mainly with a guy from Leamington Spa who'd come with me and is a great fighter.

Taking it as a learning curve I predict that a month of so of this group and I'll feel confident enough to try one of the more experienced Combat classes in another KMM venue.

On Thursday I attend the Leamington Spa class with the Chief Instructor like I've done for over 2 years and as usual it's a lot of fun and hard work. By tailoring the lessons around what works for me, I feel a lot less anxious about what I'm doing and believe therefore that when I gear up for my next grading in 6 months or a year, I'll be a lot more into it than if I'd simply ploughed ahead without trying different things out.

This reluctance and discomfort around the fighting side of Krav has bugged me for months, but now I've found a way to deal with it gradually and get up to speed. If shock and immersion therapy don't work…then it's time to look for another way of getting from A to B.

---

*\*\* In one venue it's the same guy. 6 feet 11 inches tall and P5.*

## The Safest Form of Travel
## Air Rage and Hijacking Seminar
## Bournemouth Airport

28th May 2015

"Be the grey man." Tuition on how to deal with disruptive and/or aggressive aircraft passengers with the added bonus of a simulated hijack on a real passenger jet. Organised by Nick Maison, KMG UK instructor level E3, who spent 14 years in the British Army with 7 as a physical training instructor including unarmed combat, and Jose Silva, level G5, from No Fear Academy who is a former Portuguese RESCOM Special Forces soldier. It promised to be a right treat. The location was Bournemouth International airport in a private training facility.

There were two groups for this, morning and afternoon and I was down for the early session starting at 10am. I got there just gone 9 o'clock and chatted with some other guys from other clubs. A lad named Carsten Mell had flown in from Cologne in Germany just to attend the seminar. He said "It looks like an interesting workshop. I fly regularly and self defence for an aircraft is a good idea."

Another guy named Garry Stacey from KMDA in Milton Keynes, stated that he came due to not being a good flyer after once getting on a flight that was caught in a storm.

A group of ladies I'd graded next to at my P4 exam were there from the Institute of Krav Maga. One said "I'm always on planes. It's good life skills."

It's always been at the back of my mind just how dangerous a passenger plane can be. I fly no-frills airlines quite regularly abroad and the cramped space and limited environment can sometimes prove stressful, especially if it's delayed for any reason. Nick Maison referred to a plane in flight as a 'sealed can', and told us in the briefing beforehand that the laws governing restraint of unruly passengers are very strict. The Tokyo Convention of 1963 gives a flight commander the power to authorise both cabin crew and passengers to restrain 'anyone who they have reasonable grounds to believe is about to commit an act which may jeopardise the safety of the aircraft'.

Once everyone was assembled Nick and Jose took us to a meeting room and introduced us to other guys assisting them, and Andrew Easton – the founding director of JARE, the company whose training facilities we would be using. They have a real Boeing 737 jet in the car park outside their offices at Bournemouth airport, with the back end and most of one wing removed for space issues. This was where we would be working.

Andrew gave us a brief introduction and a list of polite

Do's and Don'ts with regard to etiquette (such as not chewing gum on board). He then introduced a lady named Julie Rushton, who would act as our 'stewardess'.

Nick and Jose then briefed us on the hijack simulation we were about to go through. He warned that this would be played as if it was real and if anyone genuinely wished for the scenario to be halted, they had to use the code word "Red" at which point everyone would stop and that person would be taken off the plane. He added that they needed this as "You're hurting me", would be simply ignored or add fuel to the fire for guys pretending to be hijackers.

I was pleasantly surprised when Nick then specifically stated that the whole point of what we were about to do was NOT to teach us techniques to disarm terrorists. We were told to blend in, do as you're told and hopefully no one would get hurt and the situation would be resolved. He then warned us that we would be shoved around and abused and nothing that happened in the next 30 minutes was to be taken personally. The final piece of advice he gave was, "If anyone wants to take on the hijackers then feel free but we WILL give you a kicking and then throw you off the aircraft."

We all had designated seats and were frisked by Nick, Jose and other instructors before we got on board. When we were all in, Julie began giving the expected speech about flight safety and a guy at the front insisted on using the toilet despite her protestations. Next thing he emerges with a balaclava on, with pepper spray and a knife that he held to Julie's throat. Orders were then barked from the rear of the craft and we turned to see more guys in balaclavas holding pistols and knives. One shouted that they were the Anti Israeli Nuclear Faction and that we were to do exactly as we were told in order to not get hurt.

Guys walked up and down the aisle barking at us shut the blinds and then to put our heads down and our hands on our knees. The lights went down and it was disorientating and scary. People then were told to stand up and move and if they didn't do it quickly enough or looked up while moving the hijackers would get angry, roughly pushing people around and shouting, "You f***ing deaf? Do you want to die?! DO AS YOU'RE F***ING TOLD!!!" I was pulled up and made to lie on the floor at the front of the aircraft in front of the 3 seats. I had the sense to keep my head down and comply with all instructions as best I could.

After a few minutes I was then ordered to stand up again and shoved back to my original seat where I was made to sit with my legs crossed. Problem was that with your hands on your head and your neck bent the position becomes painful after a short while. I didn't move and just tolerated it but all around me I could hear the occasional,

"YOU F***ING LOOKING AT ME, I BLOW YOUR F***ING BRAIN OUT!!! DON'T LOOK AT ME."

Another thing that happened a few times was people caught giggling and the terrorists going mental, accusing them of finding the whole thing funny and getting incredibly aggressive until an apology was given. Another event was that one of them would shout something like, "Do you all want to live?" and we were forced to shout "YES" repeatedly.

Next thing I was poked in the shoulder by a pistol and one hijacker asked, "What's your name?" Remembering to keep my head down I answered and he snapped, "Look at me when you're talking to me!" and I raised my face to find he was wearing a headlamp shining right in my eyes. I managed to give straight answers of my full name, age and where I was from before he then moved on. Something that was quite chilling was we could hear the hijackers talking to some of the women and the girl next to me was asked if she was married, had kids or a boyfriend. When she replied no the guy said, "Don't believe you, good looking girl like you. When this is over I'm taking you out for a drink."

I was then moved to the wing section and made to kneel down and the actor whispered in my ear, "Shout like you're being beaten". I gave it a good minute of so of pleading and wailing before he then chose someone else.

With the lights down, the yelling and screaming and being ordered to not look up, the whole thing was totally disorientating with no real sense of who was around you, chinks of light through the closed shutters in the darkness and the acrid stench of sweat and bodies. I had no sense of time and after what seemed ages a smoke grenade went off in the plane and actors playing armed police swarmed on board and arrested the terrorists. I had heard about etiquette during sieges such as Columbine or the SAS storming the Iranian embassy in 1980 so kept my hands on my head and didn't look up as they shouted that we had been saved. They then told us to stand up and head for the door.

This is about as close as I ever want to come to a real hijack situation. The feelings of impotence, helplessness and fear are palpable, even in a training scenario. I complied and followed all instructions and as a result wasn't really bullied. However, none of the instructors pulled any punches during this and when we headed for the classroom after for the debrief, Nick stated that they had deliberately done things to provoke anger and shock, such as making a woman lie down and then making a guy lie on top of her. He asked how that would make you feel if it was your mother, wife or daughter. They had also slapped a few people and split couples up. Jose had apparently ordered a guy to take a swing at him who was then dragged up the back of the plane where they pretended to beat him up.

Nick reiterated that the purpose of that was so we'd know how it felt to be in that situation and that they were not teaching us how to disarm terrorists.

He repeated the 'grey man' line and it was clear to me that in a situation such as this, where the hijackers are armed with guns, organised, and know what they're doing, that there is NOTHING you can do except comply and hope for the best.

We then returned to the plane and moved on to dealing with disruptive passengers. This was common sense stuff on how to cope if for example the person next to you freaks out or becomes violent. The techniques change depending what seat you're in. Mostly if they are by the window it's a lot of pinning the arms and backing out while dropping the trays down to create a temporary barrier. You are also told that shouting for help is fundamental so people will know you're not the troublemaker and to bang the "call steward" button if you can as you move away. We worked with just hands and feet and then with knives. In a confined space you need to be constantly aware of what is around you, although the automatic Krav reflex of 'scanning' when breaking off is largely unnecessary in this type of set-up. Jose also pointed out during instructions that punching someone repeatedly in the head who is agitated but sitting next to you, might not be the best option as if the flight is full you will still have to sit next to them for the remainder of the journey. He extolled the virtues of simply reasoning verbally or using "softer" tactics such as restraint rather then belting someone to make them calm down.

We then tried a few gun and knife disarms for an actual hijack situation which it was emphasised were only to be used if the opportunity arose. One was if you are sitting down and a hijacker walks past with the gun in their hand. You disarm and bang them in the crotch with it, before standing up.

Another was if someone is standing over you in your seat, with a knife to your throat. This was the same technique as a standing knife threat but with the first punch being thrown while you are still seated.

An interesting instruction was how to deal with someone walking towards you in the aisle and pushing you. You let them shove twice then on the 3rd time you spin them around by pushing one shoulder and scooping the other arm. As they spin you then grab them round the neck and push hard into their lower back with your hand. Result is that the person is prostrate on the floor and can then be pinned down very easily.

When our time was up we left the aircraft to see the afternoon group waiting on the tarmac. We posed with them for a communal photo in front of the jet and then sorted ourselves out to go home.

This was a unique experience and both instructional plus a lot of fun. I thoroughly enjoyed myself and learned a great deal. I have non Krav friends who were cynical on what we could be taught with regard to dealing with hijackers, with comments about Liam Neeson or Bruce Willis flying around. Reassuring in the extreme was that the Air Safety Workshop was completely grounded in common sense and reality. Nick Maison went to pains to point out that compliance is the best way to deal with a hijack and the techniques we were taught were mainly for when there was no other alternative or to deal with the much lower level threat of an unruly passenger.

Garry Stacey told me after that it was an "Awesome experience, anyone who is planning to fly should do this seminar."

One student said "A huge amount of fun, but best of all I learnt some great Krav. The instructors were excellent and I'd definitely attend another if they held Air Safety Workshop 2!"

Much enjoyed and I really hope this one flies again.

# Biting the Bullet: Eyal Yanilov KMG World Tour 2015
## Hengrove Leisure Centre, Bristol

1st June 2014

Bartosz, the chief instructor of Krav Maga Midlands was super keen for us to attend this one. A chance to be coached by the master himself, Eyal Yanilov. Trained by the founder of Krav Maga, Imi Lichtenfeld, Eyal has been involved in Krav Maga since 1974 when he was 15 years old. He now heads up the global HQ of KMG and holds the grade of Master level 3/ Expert level 8.

This was a chance that would rarely be repeated and with the 40th anniversary tour going round the world it was clear that the opportunity to take a seminar with the main man was not something to pass up.

Most of my club were heading to Bristol, including Bartosz and another KMM instructor Al, so I booked that one too, even though there was the opportunity to meet Eyal at London the day before. Driving to Hengrove Leisure Centre was easy, although a possible omen for the day was me killing a pigeon on the M5 motorway. It hit the windscreen and when I looked in the mirror there was a storm of feathers raining down on the road.

When I got there there, were guys from clubs all over the UK including Wales, northern England and also an independent, non-KMG club called Krav Maga Bristol City Centre. After booking in at reception I found out that over 120 people would be attending this session.

Jose Silva the head of No Fear Academy said, "It's an experience for students to train with Eyal. Instructors can train with him every six months or so, but for students it is a special opportunity."

I spoke to Kelly, the chief instructor at KMG Bristol Krav Maga who said he was "Waiting to see the main man in the flesh."

Bartosz himself said to me, "I'm looking forward to taking some pictures of you guys training with Eyal."

We kicked off at 12pm and Jon Bullock, head of KMG UK introduced us to Eyal who had turned 55 two days before. Eyal greeted us with a brief recap of the history of his time in Krav, including the fact that he came to Hengrove Leisure Centre 15 years ago where the seminar was 6 or 7 people.

During this introduction we were startled by a voice loudly going "F**K OFF YOU BUNCH OF PRICKS!!!" and turned to see two fairly big blokes in the spectators area to the rear of the sports hall. Initially regarding this as part of the set up, it then became unnerving and embarrassing as the language got worse when Jon Bullock approached the two guys to ask them to leave. Eyal stood silently watching, while one threw a drink (plus the container) at

Jon. Amongst the swearing and masturbatory hand gestures it appeared the two unwelcome guests didn't like Krav, thought we were all a bunch of morons and offered Jon outside. They left, the door was slammed behind them and Jon said "Sorry about that, but we are in Bristol" and there was nervous laughter from all of us. Unsettling and not the way to start off such a great day. At this point I'd decided that they were Chavs from the local boozer who thought they were tough and were trying to get a reputation by threatening a room containing over 100 Krav practitioners plus the highest ranked Krav instructor in the world.

Eyal complimented Jon on his verbal reasoning and continued talking until the same two guys then re-emerged from the fire exit at the opposite end, dressed in what looked like bomb disposal gear.

They were wearing the Bullet Men suits. Huge padded, black outfits that clip together via groin guards, torso shields and 360 degree helmets covering head and neck. The idea is that you can go hammer and tongs on these blokes and it won't matter due to the heavy shielding. Same foul language and threats of abuse, with one holding a plastic knife. Jon took Eyal by the arm and led him off the mats while we all laughed (personally I was more relieved the two guys had proved to be actors) and Alan Dennis, instructor of Elite Krav Maga Midlands, took them on. He ordered them to back off and was met with more vitriolic threats so booted the first guy in the face who went down immediately and then took on the second, subduing him with kicks, elbows and punches. We gave a round of applause once it was done and Jon then stated that at the end of the seminar, 10 people would be chosen by Eyal and offered the opportunity to fight the Bullet Men in front of everyone else!

Warming up was fun with 120 people in one room. A couple of instructors were walking around taking photos and it was funny as we jogged round seeing them trying to avoid the stampede while getting a few snapshots in. Once the blood had started to flow we then moved on to some stretching with Eyal demonstrating a two person co-operation of one person lying on their back, raising and bending their legs and another sprawling against their feet and doing push ups.

This required co-ordination and timing (not to mention a strong core) and Eyal proved to have a good sense of humour when he opened his legs for one stretch and said to the guy demonstrating with him, "If you fall now, turn your head to the side." Again more laughter and people were really getting into the whole thing.

We practiced kicks and punches, including combinations and then moved to bag work on strike shields. First of all it was strikes with the forearm at a 90 degree angle and then Eyal demonstrated front kicks and then how to perform a roundhouse kick while 'bailing out' (moving to the side and out of the channel of the opponent). We then formed groups of 3 and took turns kicking hell out the bags. Eyal was walking around checking on us and stopped to have a quiet word with me about moving my hips correctly when kicking.

Moving on to knives it then became clear just how skilled Eyal Yanilov is. I'd heard it said that he moves like a dancer but a more accurate description would be that he moves like a Terminator dancing. Very flexible and bendy but you can see the power in his moves and the accuracy of his footwork. The partners he used (usually instructors) were sometimes forcibly moved back when he threw defensive blocks and counter attacks when challenged with a knife. It was also clear that he wasn't going as hard as he could if he'd wanted to. The previous instruction on high kicks to the chest, roundhouse kicks while bailing and punching were then woven into the knife defences as we learned about keeping away with a good body defence (getting away from the blade) while retaliating with kicks to vulnerable areas (chest, face or groin) on our opponents.

There was also some floor work involved, which was how to respond when someone tries a straight stab to the chest and you are on the ground. This included the 90 degree angle forearm defence and then kicking to the knees, face and groin while getting up aggressively to defend yourself.

A pause, while Eyal taught us a focusing technique in order to remain calm during stressful situations. He said as a fighter you need to remain focused. It consisted of sitting with your spine straight, head facing forwards, and linking your hands with the thumbs together. He said to gently raise your hands to your chest, inhaling to the count of 4 and then pause for 2 more seconds. You don't move your head to look down at your hands, but simply move your eyes. He then said to lower your hands to the count of 8. This proved to work very well, as I could feel the adrenalin and stress (not to mention fatigue) getting put away, so I could carry on with a fresh set of energy.

Eyal then got us to pause for some further instruction on one of the fundamental principles of Krav which is to not get too involved and to just clear out if you think you are in danger. He said to do knife defences on our opponents and once we got the knife off our partner we were to make our way to the nearest corner of the room and to pretend to check for stab wounds. The idea being that you need to put your safety before everything else, including standing your ground.

I was partnered with my KMM instructor Al and he had a great kick on him, which meant it was hard to get near enough to try and poke him with the blade.

Eyal then called for a 10 minute break and said that when we came back we should put on the plain white T-shirts that we'd been asked to bring, over the top of our club T-shirts.

Once we got back (about 20 minutes later, to which Eyal quipped, "That was a Mediterranean ten minutes.") the significance of the large number of Katie Price red lipsticks on a table became apparent. We were told to smear the lipstick on the training knife blades but not on ourselves. This was to prove just how easy it is to get stabbed and why proper knife defence, a clear head and common sense ALL matter. When we started doing this, it did indeed show just how simple it is to get the blade touching you, no matter how skilled or aggressive or tight your defence is. I was first up with the blade and managed to get Al with a few swipes, despite his long reach and mule-like kicks to my chest, groin and knife arm. When we switched I just kept backing off and bailing out, quite often colliding with other people but trying to avoid the knife.

Eyal then called a halt and Jon Bullock addressed us all. He asked the room, "Right, who thinks this is a competition?" and two guys across the hall raised their hands. After a pause Jon then continued with, "There's a reason you are the only people in this room with your hands up. This is NOT a competition; it's about putting into practice the skills you have been taught today, including common sense. Some of you are going at it like Filipino knife fighters." There was a ripple of laughter and Eyal then reiterated that we were to try and avoid the blade and rely on situational awareness and keeping distance.

Off we went again and as my energy started flagging, me and Al managed a few more attacks on each other, our T-shirts slowly starting to look like we'd been kissed by the Tasmanian devil during one of its feeding frenzies.

When they called a halt, we knew this was almost the end and as we sat and wiped the sweat from our eyes, people were being approached by Eyal and quietly spoken with before getting up and moving to the mats in the middle of the room. These were the privileged guys who were going to get the chance to fight the Bullet Men from the start of the seminar. As the spaces were filled I counted nine people and looked up to find Eyal standing over me. Smiling he asked, "Do you want to do it?" and I think I replied "Oh yes!" before moving quickly to take up the final 10th place.

I was supremely nervous but also felt honoured to have been personally chosen by Eyal for this opportunity. We sat on the mats until called up to meet the Bullet Men and while the other 110 guys got some water we took off our lipstick and sweat smeared white T-shirts and we were briefed on what to do and what to expect.

We stood in a line and were told about verbal reasoning and not to worry because Alan Dennis would be our coach and would be behind us the whole time, whispering in our ear and once we went 'hands on' with the Bullet Men we were to go full power, but stop fighting when the whistle was blown. We were shown the correct stance for verbal reasoning (feet in a fighting stance, hands up with palms out, no finger pointing as that's aggressive). The whole idea of this exercise was to see the effects of adrenalin and how people react in stressful situations. The other students and instructors were sat grouped in a horse shoe shape around the square of mats in the middle of the room. By now the word "nervous" wouldn't have done justice to how I felt but I tried to remain cold faced as we moved over.

I took the first position of the 10 of us and then Jon Bullock said from the other end of the line, "This end will probably go first" meaning I would be last and have to watch the other 9 go through the mill. There were various levels and abilities amongst us, including Ken Garriques of Krav Maga Bristol City Centre who is Expert 1.

The best way to describe the Bullet Men is that they look like the demented offspring of a Chav and a Dalek. The whole thing is like being attacked by a very angry baddy from an episode of Doctor Who. Worst part is that you can't see their faces, meaning there's no way to read expression or try and emote with the other person and the only clues as to whether they will kick off is their verbal aggression, fruity language and lack of respect for personal space. The other students were told to keep quiet during the scenarios until we went 'hands on' at which point they were to cheer us on and shout advice such as "kick him" or "use your elbows".

The first guy up was introduced and got a round of applause. Alan Dennis whispered in his ear and he stood waiting for the Bullet Man to approach. He'd clearly been instructed to be verbally aggressive because as soon as the Bullet Man spoke to him he responded with "F***K OFF!" It quickly went to fisticuffs with us all cheering and shouting encouragement. The student picked up the bullet man around the waist and dumped him on the mat and then proceeded to straddle him and punch him in the head until the whistle went and Jon and Alan pulled him away. Really good effort and everyone was impressed. One by one the students went up, with new scenarios each time and Ken Garriques having to take on both Bullet Men at the same time.

When it finally got to my turn I was by now beyond nervous. The room was quiet until Alan introduced me and I got a round of applause. I deliberately avoided looking at anyone from my own club and wished I could try the hand raising & breathing technique from earlier.

Alan whispered that I was to challenge the Bullet Men straight away, loudly and aggressively. He held the back of my T-shirt and I moved towards them. One told me to "F**K OFF!!" right off the bat, while the other, unhelmeted Bullet Man was approaching from my other side. I realised quickly they were trying to bracket me so after one more verbal warning was ignored I kicked the helmetless one in the groin and the fully protected one then jumped on me, knocking me down on the mats. We were sprawling and rolling around while the spectators went mental, shouting for me to hit the guy and one woman yelling "HIT HIM IN THE BOLLOCKS!"

While I was on top, he pinned me with his arms and legs, yanking my T-shirt up and trying to get it over my face.

I was trapped but managed to get one hand free and repeatedly punched him in the head, (while struggling to hammer his crotch with my other fist). Then the whistle went and I was pulled off him by Alan.

A great feeling of achievement to have done this, especially in front of Master Eyal himself, plus my own club and instructors. We were then asked by Jon to describe to the others how we felt both before and after we went in. My reply was "Bad, as I had to watch everyone else do it first, but it's a good feeling after." Alan said it was interesting to see all of us go from 0 to 10 in an instant once the fighting started.

We then got our certificates, shook Eyal's hand and took some photos before moving away to change into a dry T-shirt and make our way out.

Ken Garriques spoke to me later and said his club is part of Krav Maga Worldwide and the only club of that organisation in the UK. His club contains about 50 people, including around 20 female practitioners. He'd wanted himself and his students to attend as Eyal had been involved with KMW back in the day. He'd approached KMG who'd said they were more than welcome to attend and Ken was very pleased with how they were accepted by everyone. He said that taking on the Bullet Men as "Unnerving but a great experience" and that he'd chatted to Eyal who'd said he was glad they were from a group he had been associated with in the past and pleased they had come. Ken's overall opinion was, "Brilliant, loved it. Great training. Lot of basic stuff, lot of stuff I hadn't trained on ever. Great time, very pleased and very honoured to have been trained by Eyal who trained with the founder of Krav Maga."

I had a chat with Eyal himself afterwards and asked him about the day.

**"When did you first do seminars in the UK?"**

"The first seminars I gave in the UK were I believe end

of 1995, early 96. The first instructor course was 97. The beginning."

**"You said the first seminar here was like 5 or 6 guys and I assume they were all men. Is that right?"**

"If I remember correctly yes. There were people who came to different seminars that we were pushing in the lower part of England."

**"Here today we have 120 people. A lot of women. E, G and P levels. In another 15 years what do you think we're going to see?"**

"Many more people. Many more experts. Many more instructors. Many more women, hopefully."

**"Any lasting impression of today?"**

"Very good. You were all training, co-operating. Nobody was doing the opposite to what I was saying so it's really good!"

## Postman Pat vs. Chav
## (or...Verbal Reasoning & Lateral Thinking Vs. Verbal Aggression & Obnoxiousness)

### 4th June 2014

Walking with my postal wagon down the road today (big red trolley thing containing the mail, all packets and my lunch) and a young man aged about 17 wearing a pair of headphones was walking on a collision course towards me. He could politely be described as 'casually dressed' with a baseball cap, grubby jeans, hoody and a screaming case of acne.

Or more accurately described as a stereotypical Chav.

At the last moment he steps to one side and I nod acknowledgment and say "Thanks mate."

He takes one earphone out and goes "What?"

I take both my earphones out and repeat "Thanks mate."

He glares at me and then sneers "Thought you'd have moved out the way for me!"

After pause I reply "Err...I'm the one pushing the big, heavy, hard-to-move-out-the-way thing."

"You f***ing prick!"

"Charming, you have a good day yeah" (I go to move away).

He glares at me, steps a couple of feet back and then says "You wouldn't be smiling if I was to take a blade to you and wipe that smile off your face."

I look back and smile again then take some mail out of the front of the wagon. "Big scary guy like you, ooh! Wouldn't want to mess with you would I?" I slam the hatch.

"No you wouldn't, if I wanted to I could have you lying on the floor in 5 seconds flat."

He is WELL out of striking distance and has his hands jammed into his front jeans pockets. His tone is flat and unthreatening and it's clear that he's simply monologuing a stream of threats that he's used times before.

I wave my hand at him. "Not talking to you any more, go away." I take a bundle of mail and go to move to the next house.

"What you say?"

"You deaf as well? F\*\*k off!"

"Seriously mate if I didn't have somewhere to be I'd lay you out right now."

He walks back so I stand on the other side of the wagon and decide on a compromise between walking off and having to actually engage with the little shit. "I'm bored of this. Tell you what…!" I put one earphone back in and hold the cable halfway up and pretend to press a button with my thumb. In my ear are AC/DC demanding to know Who Made Who?

"What, you gonna call the old bill or something?"

I smile and hold up my hand for quiet and then pretend to have the following conversation:

"Voice activate number 5. (Pause). Hello, police please. (Longer pause). Hello mate, yes can I have police assistance to outside 23 Letsby Avenue, Leamington Spa. IC3** male, about 17 years of age is threatening me and being verbally abusive. I'm a postman so I'm concerned about the integrity of the mail."

The Chav continues to just stare blankly at me.

"My name, (false laugh)? No I can't tell you that as he's standing here listening to me. Ok, thanks. See you in 5."

I pretend to hang up and say brightly, "Whatever you're thinking of doing you've got about 5 minutes so be quick."

He steps back again and mumbles, "If I didn't have to be somewhere I'd just stand here and wait for them, I'm not afraid of the filth."

"Good for you, that's the spirit. You have a good day yeah."

He slopes off up the road.

Job done.

-------------------------------------------

** *Black.*

## The Slightly Kravvy Bit of the Holiday

8th July 2014

Just winding up a wonderful 4 weeks in Plakias, Crete, Greece. Plakias is a fishing village in the south of the island with an official indigenous population of 130. However from May to October it's a haven for backpackers, returnees and ex pats who swell the residents to over 4000.

My father retired out here in 1996 and I try to spend at least a month a year here; going scuba diving, swimming, cliff jumping, hiking...and of course drinking till about 5am.

Some time ago a newbie at my club asked me if I'd ever had to use Krav Maga in real life. Answer was "No" as the only time the opportunity occurred it was in a bar brawl (ironically at a Plakias reunion in London) and I got my arse handed to me, mainly as I'd been doing Jaeger bombs and had sunk about six pints of lager when things kicked off. I'd also recently passed P2 which made the experience all the more humiliating.

This summer I can now finally answer "Yes" to that question, due to the unwanted attention of a lecherous and drunken bloke in a disco bar.

Me and a mate plus the girls we were dating went up

to Ostraco, which has two floors, the upper one being used for dancing with a great balcony and the owner/ manager Iannis playing video tracks to dance to via a massive cinema screen at one end. I had had a lot to drink and was dancing merrily with my mates when I felt a pair of hands grab my chest from behind and start squeezing gently.

Assuming it was my pal Eve, who has a habit of doing that, I played along for a few seconds before glancing down to see the hands were far from dainty and decidedly hairy.

I broke the guy's hold by grabbing his hand and spinning round, attempting to wrist lock him. Being drunk I fumbled it and managed what could be best described as an "index finger lock". I stood there glaring at him while holding his finger and he squealed:

"NO DON'T DO THAT! DON'T DO THAT! DON'T DO THAT!"

I extended my other hand for a handshake (while still holding his finger and giving it a slight twist) and replied:

"Don't think we've been introduced. My name's Lance. DON'T do that again!"

He shook my hand, I let his finger go and him and his mate walked out.

I told Iannis the owner who looked furious and went "WHERE IS HE?!!" but I assured him that it wasn't a big deal and the guy had gone.

Very glad that I actually reacted to that the way I'd been trained to and that despite being three sheets to the wind my first instinct was to do what my Krav instructor had told me.

## Common Sense Before Valour

13th July 2014

For the last 4 weeks I've been in Plakias. A wonderful holiday resort in Crete, Greece that my father retired to about 17 years ago. Officially it's a fishing village with an indigenous population of about 150. Unofficially it's a party town from May to October where people go to have a lot of F.U.N.

When I set off I had every intention of visiting a Krav Maga club in Athens on the mainland of Greece and training for one session with a club there. This was all arranged via e-mail before I set out but then life got in the way. The Greek KMG director was at the International Director's meeting in Israel for the first chunk of my vacation and after that my brother got sick so that didn't occur (but will either later on this year or next summer when I go back).

My brother is into martial arts, holding a black belt in Judo and a blue belt in Jiu Jitsu. He also boxes, so set up a makeshift punch bag outside my dad's apartment, hanging from one of the wooden beams, and we had the grand total of TWO sessions on that before the hangovers began to conquer my desire to remain Kravvy.

I'd also vowed I'd continue my regime of 70 inclined

push ups every day and 100 abdominal crunches. Happened the first day only.

Reality is, that unless you are very focused and seriously "into" getting and keeping super fit, a holiday is not the place to try and keep up a training schedule.

I spent a month drinking heavily nearly every day; doing shots like they were going out of style; eating ice cream for pudding meal; gobbling down a full English breakfast about 4 days a week; wolfing down a pitta gyro at least once every 2 days (a kebab with chips in it); and having hangovers that made me contemplate genocide. I did virtually no exercise (couple of scuba dives, some swimming and a lot of walking) and would sleep in till about lunchtime most days

Bottom line is that I'm now officially unfit. As much as I want to go back to Krav and train with my club again, I'm also well aware that my body needs just a little TLC before I throw myself back into this. My chief instructor Bartosz is one of the best there is, and being that good he expects a commitment from his students that I'm normally happy to give. Last year though, I came back from Plakias after a month of doing whatever the hell I liked, and nearly puked during the warm up...about 5 minutes into the session.

So this year, I've got a different plan.

On the plane from Crete to London I ordered a cup of

tomato soup and a pot of lentils with spicy couscous (menu option 5), even though I was salivating at the thought of a bacon and cheese hero sandwich, a cup of filter coffee and a Twix chocolate bar (menu option 2).

I landed back in England yesterday morning at 2am (Saturday 12th July) and slept like the dead until about 11am once I got home. I had bran flakes for breakfast, and made some soup and had a fruit smoothie for lunch and dinner. That night I chilled out in front of the TV with season 2 of "Sons of Anarchy" and again slept like the recently deceased until 11am today. I went for a bike ride of 5 or so miles (about half the distance I usually go) and came back and had a cup of soup for lunch.

I know guys who hurl themselves into Krav at every given opportunity, even if hungover or ill. Problem is that that usually invokes further issues and even possibly prolonged absence from training due to making their bodies feel a hell of a lot worse. Having trained while "under the weather" I know how you must feel at least 95% fit in order to gain anything from sports, especially something as cardio-based as Krav Maga.

My body is different now to how it was a month ago. I've gained about half a stone, I have a lot less stamina and my endurance is low. Not to mention that anyone using the toilet after me currently needs to take a canary in a cage in there with them.

Either later this week or early next week, I will return to my club and get stuck in. I'm itching to go back there now, but won't. One of the things Krav has showed me is that sometimes it pays to be patient and not run but walk.

So that one may walk in peace. Not fall to pieces.

## (Under) Stand Your Ground

### 22nd July 2014

A few short years ago, before I was into Krav, and for sometime after I would be stubborn if faced with confrontation. I couldn't fight. Hadn't been able to all my life...but I would stand my ground and get knocked down or worse if necessary JUST to prove that I wasn't a coward.

My attitude at the time was: "You may be able to punch me out, you may be able to beat me up but I'm gonna show you that I'm not afraid."

In 2011 me and some friends got caught having a midnight swim in a pool in Athens. It was my friend Julia's 27th birthday and she loved the pool and spent most days there swimming and sunbathing. Turns out that Athenians loathe trespassers and so the owner climbed out of his chalet with baseball bat and threatened me with it, punctuated with lots of swearing and grunts of "malaka!" which means "wanker" and is about the most insulting thing you can say to someone else in Greek.

I was monumentally angry at this, and being drunk told him to go fuck himself. I then added "We'll leave OK but there's no need for THAT!" I beckoned the others over to get out the pool while the angry man stood there glaring at me. As my friends gathered their stuff he suddenly lost it and span around as Julia bent over to get her purse and whacked her hard across the arse with the bat. It made an audible "crack!" and I tried to get in between them shouting "What the fuck are you doing?!!"

Next thing I know I'm on my back as another guy had just punched me in the head. I leapt back up yelling "DON'T HIT THE WOMEN!" and again stood in between them. My friends bolted (including, depressingly, the only other male from the group who was the first to run for the sanctuary of the road) while I stood there, palms up facing these two until I was certain that my pals had gone.

Bottom line was. It ended badly, I got knocked down, but I had stood my ground and for that I felt proud.

Problem is....had I simply backed off when I saw the bloke with the bat. Had I not lost my temper and sworn at him. Had I not shouted at him and then stood my ground then he probably wouldn't have lashed out the way he did. Athenians HATE trespassers and his overly aggressive posture and attitude were possibly just for show. I later found out that with no entrance gate, this pool gets people taking drunken swims at 3am at least once a week.

Now, with three years-ish of Krav Maga under my patch and the rank of P4 (stick defences resit pending) I find it much easier to suppress my ego and pride and think of a common sense option for what is happening in front of me. Recently I got threatened by some gobby shitbag in the street. Instead of getting into a slanging match and possible fisticuffs I pretended to call the police via my headphones and the lad buggered off once he thought the "filth" were on the way.

This year in Crete some guy groped me on the dance floor of a local disco bar. I twisted his hand away as I'd been taught and instead of freaking out or breaking his nose, simply shook his other hand (while still holding his finger) and told him not to do it again.

Ultimately Krav at its essence is about NOT fighting. It's about avoiding confrontation unless you have absolutely no choice. It doesn't make you a coward for not fighting. Instead it realigns your sense of what is important, necessary and appropriate in a situation.

Wading in fists flying and yelling may look impressive but is likely to get you killed.

## Junior Safe Krav Maga

24th July 2014

*Russell Brotherston is the instructor at Junior Safe Krav Maga (JSKM), with two clubs based in Stratford-upon-Avon, and Warwick in England. The Stratford branch opened in September 2013, with children aged 6 to 15. In May 2014, a second class opened in Warwick with children from ages 6 to 12 enrolling, many of which have parents or relatives who are Krav Maga practitioners.*

I arrived at Urban Sports Fitness in Warwick on a hot Monday afternoon in June to find a lovely room floor to floor with mats, where shoes are forbidden. Russell made it clear that the purpose of junior Krav Maga is to teach the kids valuable tools to help them cope with such issues as attempted abduction, physical bullying or even being attacked by several other children at the same time.

At around 4.50pm the first students arrived. Eager and smiling they had on their blue JSKM t-shirts and were immediately running around, laughing and repeating warm up exercises that Russell had shown them in the previous weeks.

They seemed super happy to be there and I chatted to Tanith and Dave Swain, parents of a little girl named Evie who is 6. Tanith said "I got Evie to come along as I wanted to give her something to do that would increase her confidence and help her to be able to defend herself."

Evie was clearly happy warming up with her friends, running around playing games and was fitting right in. Dave told me "They learn through playing. Russell makes it fun to the kids and it's a game for them."

Another parent said "My kids wanted to do it after knowing I was doing it plus seeing You Tube videos of kids doing Krav in the Netherlands. With my youngest it's a confidence building exercise as he was bullied physically at school."

As the kids continued arriving Russell let them run around for a little while, explaining that children this young have almost limitless energy and it's good to let them work up a sweat straight away so they can focus throughout the whole lesson.

When it came to the first bow it was way more fun than the one we do at adult Krav. The kids all knelt with Russell (most of them grinning wildly) and after a brief "Hello" they leaned forward, beat the mats with their fists and yelled "KIDA!" as loudly as they could.

Russell was grinning too, clearly enjoying himself as he got the kids into pairs. He said they had to hold their partner down for five seconds, and then swap. After a few attempts at this they moved on to trying to flip someone over who was lying face down. The twist was that their partner was roaming the mats trying to flick people and if attacked the recumbent child had to yell for assistance. They seemed to really enjoy this and stuck at if for a while before a water break and then moved on to pile ups and then to bear hugs.

The main differences became apparent here as the purpose of the defence from a bear hug in JSKM works on the assumption that an adult will be the one trying it and is potentially attempting to carry a child away. Russell put on a groin guard, shin pads and full-face helmet and the kids went berserk, lashing out with elbows and kicks when picked up. Russell also told them to "Run and tell a grown up what just happened and how you feel about it" immediately after escaping.

I glanced across to see one little girl, red faced and grinning from ear to ear while jumping up and down excitedly as Russell spoke to her group.

As the lesson progressed the students then moved to a pressure drill. They had to run around while two people threw spongey bags at them. If hit they then had to stand with their eyes closed and wait while Russell roamed the mats and would grab one of them in a bear hug and lift them up. The kids seemed to really get into this, with little Evie kicking Russell a couple of times in the head when he turned her upside down.

When it was all over the kids (by now beetroot-faced and very sweaty) were lined up again and did the closing "KIDA!" with just as much, if not more, enthusiasm as the first one. They then moved to their parents to get a drink and were talking super fast to mum and/ or dad about what they'd just done.

Afterwards I spoke to Russell.

**"So what do you think kids this young can gain from doing Krav Maga?"**

"Confidence is a huge, huge part of it. One girl today wasn't very confident to start with but all she needed was a little bit of encouragement. She was very anxious about being picked up. We adapted and showed her more techniques to not let someone do it in the first place. It's still the same basic lesson but adapted so that she doesn't get scared and gets slowly more confident."

**"How different is this to the Krav Maga you teach adult practitioners?"**

"Krav Junior is very different. It's a lot more game based as their attention span is completely different to the adults. You can only spend about a minute talking about something before they start jostling and pushing each other and moving about. With children you turn it into games and when they are one on one that's your teaching opportunity. It's a lot more fast paced. I get more tired than in the adult classes definitely (laughs). They keep going and going. They're like Duracell bunnies. Some can be a little bit naughty but I think you need that leeway to allow them to be a little mischievous. It has to be fun for them, if you're too serious they won't enjoy it and they won't want to come and it'll be like a lot of martial arts where they stand in a line and do the same things over and over again. We threw a few things into the pressure drill that they've never learned, things they don't really know.

Kids are lot more intuitive that way. Adults have a tendency to try and overthink things while kids will just start hitting."

## For Granted

26th July 2014

Something that I've always known, but kind of forgot, was that fitness is something you constantly have to sustain. Unless you're 18 years old you can't retain a six pack stomach and big pecs unless you strive for them.

Recently I spent a month where I drank heavily, partied regularly and ate lots of saturated fat, red meat and generally unhealthy but delicious stuff. I also drank at least 5 pints of lager a day (and usually more) and did a ridiculous amount of shots.

I'm not boasting about any of this but getting back into Krav Maga has been tortuous to say the very least. I deliberately left it for nearly a week before I went back and felt like shit all through my first session.

The following night I went to a seminar my club was holding and felt a bit better, although my concentration was wavering. Last night I went again and while I managed to get stuck in, my breathing felt like acid coming up through my esophagus and when I tried an abdominal exercise I found my core stability had been shot to hell by the lack of exercise in the previous weeks.

Someone told me that if you are at a reasonable or high level of fitness it will take ONE MONTH of training to regain every WEEK that you didn't train.

Before I went away there were several lovely moments of Kravdom that made me feel like a warrior king.

For example...

At the Solihull class the instructor Al, got us to do a cardio based warm up exercise where one bit was inclined push ups.

I did more and finished faster than ANYONE else on my group of 5, even though every other lad in the team was at least 20 years younger than me.

Another time a young bloke turned up for an induction and had to leave to throw up halfway through due to being unfit. I asked him his age and smiled to myself when he said he was 25, eighteen years my junior.

So...all that wonderful fitness and cardio based badassery has now gone for a holiday of its own. While I can still fight I tire much quicker, sweat much more profusely and my chest burns with a Sahara like intensity once heavy moving and striking are involved.

Something I took for granted (without even meaning to) was my fitness and now I'm paying for it big time.

Knowing you are strong and fit is a wonderful feeling. Wanting to power vomit due to running for 5 minutes is totally crap.

Bring on the rocket and baby leaf salads and my trusty bicycle.

# The Bonus Material

### 30th July 2014

Like a decent Blu-Ray, Krav Maga has a lot of supplementary material thrown in. Not only do I now feel more confident physically but I've recently realised just how much "good" stuff I get thrown in for free.

For example...

1. Feeling useful

I like to feel useful. I like to feel I've helped someone. I also like to reassure those who look like they need it. At inductions this is entirely possible due to the newbies that turn up. You know the scene. Non club t-shirt, no groin guard and so queasy they look like they are about to audition for the X Factor. A simple introduction and handshake seems to be appreciated and I try to partner newbies during the initial part of the lesson (at inductions with KMM we focus on the basic strikes for a while). I also attempt to be reassuring. Something I used to do and I see other people do if they're new, is to apologise whenever they hit their partner or successfully put them on the floor. E.g. During "Try and touch your partner's chest while they try and prevent it" you can hear a lot of embarrassed "Sorrys" and "You OK?" when someone gets through the other's guard. Also during headlock releases you can see the looks of unease on inductionees as bodies thud to the floor after having their faces grabbed. Again, being reassuring to those who aren't used to this can work wonders and put them at ease.

Best way to some this up would be "Feel free to kick my groin, it's protected. If you aim for my leg to try and be nice then that's gonna hurt!"

2. Self confidence

This gets a boost due to the longevity of me doing Krav for 3 years. If you spar with someone you know is better than you, and even ONCE manage to land a hard roundhouse or right hook...then you feel great. I've never been a fighter and being able to face guys much better than me and, win or lose, walk away after touching gloves with your opponent it makes you feel much taller. Feeling that the techniques are coming together into a coherent pattern that you have incorporated into your muscle memory is cause for jubilation.

This ripples out to other areas of my life so I am less agitated in social or even work situations as I feel I can try more things and give them a good go.

3. Paranoia Killer

I've always been a bit paranoid. A mixture of the beta blocker and Krav have made me realise that the world isn't out to try and hurt or upset me and, as Imi Lichtenfeld once said, "So that one may walk in peace."

Being able to walk down the main street without feeling anxious, nervous or (at night when the drunks are out like something from The Walking Dead) scared...is a great feeling.

4. Ego Compacter

Another thing I've always had is a big ego. Not simply for self promotion but the desire that if something happened that was unjust or unfair then I HAD to do something.

I joined the police in 2004 because I wanted to be a hero (and resigned in 2008). I would see injustice and wade in. Like Liam Neeson tracking his kidnapped daughter in the movie Taken, I didn't have a "next step". I'd simply wade in, with almost no fighting ability, an average size body and an ego that wanted to crush all bullies and perpetrators of injustice.

After doing Krav for over 36 months I can now weigh up a situation and walk away or try and defuse it verbally...without feeling like a pansy. I recently had an argument with a friend of mine who had drunk 6 bottles of Greek raki and was telling the girl I was dating that she "deserved better than Lance."

Attempts to tell him to back off were met with the response "You want to get into it with me? Coz it won't last long!" and due to my obvious anger, my date got upset. I stayed calm and vowed to speak to my mate when he was sober. Next day he had no memory of the incident and was embarrassed and apologetic. Had my older self been there, there would have been at the very least some pushing and shoving, followed by the two hulking sons of the Greek owner of the bar we were drinking in, breaking it up and asking one or both of us to leave.

Krav is about avoiding the confrontation unless necessary. Best comparison was an incident 10 years ago in Moldova when a local guy insulted the woman I was with, Helen, and called her a whore for drinking with foreigners. I was very drunk and followed him into a room (where about 4 of his mates were waiting for him) and demanded he say sorry to Helen. Next thing the barman took my gently by the arm and pulled me away.

I felt that honour was satisfied but Helen said to me the next day "I wasn't bothered by him. He was just some stupid guy. Moldavian men sometimes carry knives or even guns. You could have got yourself killed and for what? To prove you are better than him?"

Avoid the fight, don't let your ego put you in the morgue.

## That "Near The End of the Summer Holidays" Feeling

3rd September 2014

After a Krav Maga grading I feel knackered but exhilarated. After all, I did it. I made the grade. On P2, 3 and 4 I came away with my body shouting abuse at me for the misery I'd put it through, but I felt A.W.E.S.O.M.E.

I might even miss the next lesson at the club and unwind with a shed load of alcohol (Guinness makes a good substitute Night Nurse) and a gallon of ice cream. The DVD relevant to that grade gets put back in the sleeve and put back on the shelf. The patch goes in the frame with its predecessors, at the corners of the certificate for my current level**

It's a wonderful feeling of having achieved something special and risen in the ranks.

It's in fact, very similar to that feeling I got when the school broke up for the summer holidays.

Six whole weeks of F.R.E.E.D.O.M to do what I wanted***, run around, stay up late and generally have F.U.N. The summer felt like it would never end. That first week would be a joyous adventure, knowing I had five more weeks after it. Weeks 2 through to 5 would be spectacular. On hols with the parents and my brother, back to play with my mates and ride my bike around town to my heart's content. No pressure.

Problem was, by week 5, once we got past Sunday I was feeling down and getting tense. After all, once that precious Monday was used up, there would not be another to replace it the week after.

The same with every day up until that horrible Monday when we went back to school.

Then I'd have to don the dreaded school uniform again and traipse up the driveway of Shitbag Comprehensive (otherwise known as Kenilworth School) to endure another term of bullying, boredom and dark sarcasm in the classroom.

But I digress...

In 4 weeks we have the Pre-Assessment Workshop for the upcoming October gradings. That "Beginning of the School Holidays" feeling is now becoming a "I'll have to go back to Maths and Chemistry" feeling.

Down to work; as many sessions a week as possible; new level's DVD on mail order; book the venue...and spend my time getting nervous.

When I took P4 I was stressed almost to ruination the entire week before the grading. Fact it was hosted by the Master level 1 Zeev Cohen didn't help my nerves overly much.

So instead of 6 weeks of riding my bike, staying up late and hanging out with my friends, I now have 6 monthly gaps of trying to remain focused instead of just riding on the euphoria of having passed a Practitioner level yet again.

Defending Against Impending Knife Threat?

Can do.

-------------------------------------------

*\*\* Apart from P4 which I have passed but haven't passed as I have to redo stick defences before I get the patch or certificate, even though the stamp is in my passport. God bless "conditional passes".*

*\*\*\* Mother and fathers' approval pending.*

# The Eternal Practitioner

### 23rd September 2014

Throughout life there are different sets of responsibilities that slot into place as we walk through the process known as "growing up."

At about 5 you have to go to school, which is a huge change from hanging out with mummy or daddy and learning the rules of how to "play" (i.e. the advent of having to share your toys and say 'please' and 'thank you'). You may later on have a younger brother or sister to look after. You will be tasked to "set an example" to the younger kids at school. You have to tidy your room. Etc.

As you move up in years you may have a part time job (in my day the ignominious delights of a paper round) and become a Prefect at school (assuming that they still guilt older kids into being unpaid supervisors for younger ones).

Your responsibilities mount up as you move ever onwards in years.

In adulthood most people find a niche that fits the life of an adult. They form relationships, make lasting friendships and get a job that pays enough to set up a mortgage. They marry, have children and then settle into the life of a fully fledged "grown up". Even later in life they pass their knowledge and wisdom (or lack of) on to the next generation of grandchildren.

Life can basically be split into 3 levels. Practitioner, Graduate and Expert.

At Practitioner level we are learning. While some things are easy to pick up; such as walking, talking and riding a bike others aren't quite so simple such as Maths, science or how to tie your shoelaces quickly. However we eventually learn and move on.

Graduate skills are based more on using the Practitioner stuff as a grounding. From basic science we move into the worlds of physics and chemistry and biology. The ability to speak is used to leapfrog into the skill of being able to express yourself through writing or learn a second language. Skills in social interaction will lead to finding a sexual partner and maybe having children. Being aware of danger will be used to become daily awareness of personal space, traffic and hazards. The lists go on.

By the time we reach the Expert levels of life, we are grounded in a full knowledge of Practitioner and Graduate skill sets. The earlier levels rarely need to be refreshed (although they do need to be, now and then) and we can pass on our judgments and experience to those who came into the world later on.

I am approaching a P5 grading, probably in December

at the P camp that Krav Maga Global are holding.

There is a part of me that wants to rest on my laurels once this is achieved and not go any further. After all, that lovely patch with its 5 bars would look much more eye catching than a G patch with only one bar...wouldn't it?

Not really...but it's tempting to remain the highest grade of Practitioner than become the lowest level of Graduate. The reasons are a mixture of fear, foreboding but mainly the knowledge that I'll have to actually start taking some responsibility in my life as I move from the P levels to levels where I will not only be eligible to take an instructor's course (regrading pending of course) but attend G camp.

The primary worry is that by stepping into big boys' pants I will be obliged to actually act like a Graduate, rather than remain an eternal Practitioner.

Sometimes growing up can be scary.

## KMM Pre Grading Workshop
## Stratford upon Avon Leisure Centre

5th October 2014

In March I took my Practitioner 4 grading in London Copperbox Arena, watched over by none other than Zeev Cohen, deputy director of KMG Global. I gained what is known as a "conditional pass", meaning I had achieved the grade of P4 by getting 73% (minimum pass is 70%), had the stamp in my passport BUT had to retake stick defences back in my own club at Krav Maga Midlands before I could get my certificate.

I didn't feel too bad as it wasn't just me. ALL the other P4 guys from my club who graded in London or Bristol had to retake one or two things before the treasured four bar patch was handed over.

KMM Chief Instructor Bartosz held the in house resits in May, but I was double booked attending Nick Maison's Air Safety seminar in Bournemouth that day.

The next available slot was the pre grading workshop in September so I waited patiently until I could finally gain my fourth.

After 6 months I knew my knowledge of what I'd learned would be shaky and I was nervous about having forgotten too much.

Not long before the national gradings, KMM hold workshops at Stratford upon Avon Leisure Centre. The last two have been run by instructors Al Natrins and Russell Brotherston and they treat each workshop with the same intensity as an actual grading.

The idea is that you work through what you will be tested on, on the grading day but with constant feedback and a debrief at the end.

There was about 15 of us this time and most were going for P1 or P2. A few new faces were on the mats as we lined up, and it was good to see them and know they were going to take the plunge and actually go for it.

After a quick warm up we split off into our relevant grades with the P1s and 2s at one end me and two others on the other side. I was with a former Russian Olympic wrestler and a Polish guy. Both are huge, hulking blokes and very powerful. The wrestler was prepping for P4 in October while the other guy was gearing up for his Graduate 1 examination (he was the first P5 student in KMM and was regarded with a sense of awe for about 6 months until other guys made the same grade).

Al and Russell got us to drill specific techniques and we got stuck in. For me this was realistically a P4 test all over again and I was conscious of having to nail techniques correctly. We concentrated on upper cuts, hooks and hammer blows and then moved on to kicks.

Tomasz gave constant advice to me and Toli, which was unexpected but turned out to be useful as he knew his stuff. I dropped my hands a few times during the kicks so Tom handed me a focus mitt and got me to hold it between my hands, meaning I couldn't drop them every time I kicked.

We moved on to the more complicated moves, including Scissor Kick which I had forgotten over the preceding 6 months and had only managed to get down properly the Thursday before.

Thankfully this was something I did well and it was reassuring to hear Tomasz grunt "Good, close" as he held the strike shield.

Doing this for four hours is grueling, however ultimately necessary as it is as close to the real thing as you will get. The last grading in March was the hardest I've ever done and it was good to see that KMM weren't pulling any punches (or kicks) in making sure we were fit for the job.

After getting through stick defences we switched to ground work. Working with guys who are nearly twice my size turned out to be a blessing, as it meant I had to do the techniques correctly or there was absolutely no way I was going to get them off me.

Me and Toli were well and truly knackered by this point (Toli had the foresight to bring 3 t-shirts and had already changed once, I'd only brought 2 so my training shirt was by now impersonating a haddock's bikini) BUT we had one more treat in store. While the P1s and 2s did ground wrestling and a zombie drill...we had to go full on at a strike pad held by one of the other guys, while the 3rd man kept trying to attack us with a knife or stick (and in the other's case a pistol). This was draining and when we finally finished we were well and truly exhausted.

As we packed up the stuff I was trying to remain aloof about asking whether I'd passed or not, but failed that charade miserably. Al said that as far as he was concerned I'd done OK but needed to convene with Russell (who was outside to drop the training gear into his car). I spent an anxious 15 minutes waiting and Al broke it to me like this:

"Well unfortunately.................we don't think you're ready for P5 but you've got P4".

As I remember it, my gratitude was punctuated by one or two swear words. A really good experience and it further reassures me that both KMM and KMG UK are 100% focused on training and testing their students at a level of high achievement.

The workshop was arduous and the following day I had bruises on various bits of my body plus a couple of beauties across my face BUT it means all the students actually know their stuff and can be proud that they are being tested by a meticulously professional organization.

I have P5 at the P Weekend in December.
Best get training again.

## Kiddy Kida

8th October 2014

Russell Brotherston, a G4 Krav Maga instructor with Krav Maga Midlands, runs Junior Safe Krav Maga/ JSKM on Mondays in Royal Leamington Spa. I have been a couple of times before, as an observer and it always looked like a lot of fun. The kids seemed to really enjoy it, Russell was clearly having the time of his life and the various KMM Krav students that were assisting him were obviously having a great time .

Russell asked me to help out last Monday and I was more than up for it as I've worked with children on and off since about 1995 teaching English and on summer camps.

The format is VERY different to adult Krav, right from the first Kida! (kneel, pound the mat as hard as you can with your fists and shout at the top of your lungs). The main emphasis is on evasion techniques and using fast force to dodge, evade or strike a stronger, bigger attacker (i.e. an adult).

When I got there a couple of the girls were running about playing Tig and wanted me to join in. This quickly degenerated into something not dissimilar to Calvinball from the cartoon strip CALVIN AND HOBBES (i.e. "The only rule is that there are no rules").

The children seemed to have the same energy as a nuclear reactor and I quickly worked up a good sweat on the mats.

At about 5pm we got sorted, Russell introduced me to the kids and had them playing a continuation of Tig but where, when I tapped them, they had to stand still and he would walk up to them and grab their arm. They had to perform the appropriate technique to get out of that and then he'd let them go.

It's been a few years since I was a pre-teen, and I'd forgotten just how competitive children can be. It was endearing to see just how fast they pelted about the room to avoid getting caught.

We then moved on to a game where their punching skills came into play and in teams of they had to run up to me or Russell and punch a strike mitt ten times, then run to the end of the room and perform a grab release, before running back so the next person could have a go. This inevitably led to lots of shouting and encouragement and both teams declaring themselves the winners at the end.

We then moved on to a game where me and Russell chased them and would then grab either their T-shirts or their wrists and not let go until they performed a decent release move. Russell demonstrated the knuckle rap release (or "knocking on the barn door") which hurts like hell if done properly, even if a little kid is doing it. To negate any pain issues, we both put MMA gloves on and then got to work. Again, this was a lot of fun and I couldn't help laughing when one 6 year old (the smallest girl in the class) simply booted me in the crotch, grinned broadly and then ran off again when I took her arm (God bless the inventor of the groin guard).

While I grabbed a quick sip of water and wiped the sweat from my brow, they were still jumping up and down ready for the next game.

Idea this time was that I had two soft strike pads and would throw them at the kids who had to try and dodge them and, if hit, stand still. Russell would walk up behind them and either bear hug them or put them in a headlock and they had to once again perform the appropriate release.

First time (and probably last) that I would ever get to impersonate Rinzler from Tron Legacy. Great time hurling the pads at the indignant students, a couple of which were very nimble and one in particular proved hardest to catch, sometimes simply jumping over the pad as I threw it at him. Picking them up again was playing havoc with my back and I vowed silently to get into some Yoga in the very near future.

Final game had me and Russell sitting on a full sized strike shield each, and each team (about five kids per group) had to try and take it off us and drag it to the back of the room. I thought this would be easy but it seems that nothing is more determined than a gang of children whose combined ages come to about 26. Within about a minute they'd managed to wrench it off me and were leaping around celebrating victory.

By the end the kids were still loving it and with a few disappointed groans they lined up for the final Kida! Every session Russell chooses two children to come and kneel next to him at the end, meaning they have shown the most determination or shone in other ways throughout the session. He chose one child and asked me to pick another. I selected a lad who was only on his second session but had got stuck in with a big grin on his face the whole way through.

I told his mum after, that his spectacles seemed like Indiana Jones's hat, as he never lost them no matter what happened.

A lot of fun had by all and a great way to educate kids to basic self defence and team work.

## Krav Maga Midlands Warzone 2 Seminar
## Stratford-upon-Avon High School

Sunday 8th November 2014

I had been looking forward to this one for over a month. Having missed Warzone 1 last year, this was the chance to learn how to disarm both pistols and automatic rifles and then face a "hostage situation" scenario at the end of the training. KMM Chief Instructor Bartosz was super keen for this event, with students from clubs as far away as Bristol, Reading and Southampton having signed up to attend.

With anticipation at it zenith, it was with much swearing and ill temper that I then got a dislocated finger during sparring two days before Warzone 2.

So...with much chuntering about the unfairness of life I was determined to go along anyway and just watch.

On the day a lot of guys were there early and seemed pretty pumped up, looking forward to the training. I spoke to Patrick Day-Childs from No Fear Academy who said "This looks awesome, really wanted to come to this."

After a warm up with the students, Bartosz and Russell moved on to demonstrating the Glock 17. They had a functioning replica version powered by gas, and would prime the pistol just before demonstrating a disarm, mainly to show that during a struggle the weapon can still fire and you need to have your techniques sorted. It also became apparent that due to the release button, the magazine can quite easily come loose in a fight. Bartosz stressed that the priority is to ensure you are safe and the area is clear, before you decide whether or not to go back for it.

The initial disarms were stuff we'd covered in class over the last few years but then the unique stuff was shown. The first method was if you are on your knees with a gunman facing you, pistol pointed at your head. The practice relies on swiftly moving the gun to one side of your face and then utilising the momentum of the gunman attempting to pull the gun free, to get to your feet. A technique from behind was then shown where it was clear you have to actually be able to feel the barrel touch the back of your skull before you react, so as you can gauge distance as you grab.

Further techniques involved being on your knees but then kicked in the chest so you are laying on your back. The gunman then sits astride your chest and there is a method to specifically deal with this and also if you are laying on your front with the pistol in the back of your head.

They then moved on to the bit I'd been looking forward to for so long, which was the AK 47 automatic rifle disarm.

The techniques are very different due to the fact that it's a long weapon so you need to take into account the shift in weight and positioning as you grab the barrel. The replicas themselves are quite heavy which adds even more realism to the actions. One positive bonus is that there's more to grab onto than with a pistol disarm. After trying that out for a good while, and switching positions Bartosz then split the guys into two big groups for the finale.

A smaller room with chairs against one wall had been set up to resemble seats on an aircraft. Two volunteers stepped outside while the others chatted nervously and then the door was kicked open and a couple of nasty looking types with AK47s and balaclavas burst in yelling "EVERYBODY DOWN ON THE FLOOR!!!" and other threats.

The idea was that in a situation such as this, if someone tries to take out a gunman/ terrorist then the others in the room absolutely HAVE to react quickly in order to neutralise the threat. In real life a gunman watching potential hostages or victims attempting to take down his partners will almost certainly react by shooting. The first group tackled the initial gunman very well, but left the second guy alone for precious seconds. After some feedback from Bartosz, two more guys stepped out and the exercise was repeated. This time the response was better with people getting thrown down in big rugby scrums. It resembled watching a soldier getting overpowered by zombies on The Walking Dead. Goz Gozwell of KMM had three guys on her but wouldn't let go of her rifle, constantly yelling "GIVE ME YOUR MONEY, I WANT YOUR MONEY!!!" refusing to accept the inevitable.

Bartosz pointed out on the debrief that in real life she would have been subjected to elbow, fists and feet into her face and body so hanging on to the gun was unrealistic. Between this and the next scenario the school caretaker came in to fiddle with the lock on the fire door. I initially thought this was due to us overrunning slightly on time but then we had one bad guy emerge through there, while the other ran in from the other side. Again, complete bedlam with bodies going down on the floor and lots of grunting and shoving.

The best bit was yet to come when the half of the group that had been left in the main hall with Russell then burst in to try and overpower the other guys. A melee of epic proportions as everyone piled in, and one guy running across the length of the room to drag a terrorist to the floor.

At the end Bartosz and Russell signed the attendance certificates. I jokingly asked if I got one for observing and Bartosz handed me mine, pre-printed days before. Everyone who had participated then lined up to get theirs, with a handshake and a round of applause and they went their separate ways.

Excellent tuition and it looked like a lot of fun. Just need to avoid any niggling injuries in time for next year's Warzone 3.

## Accident Waiting to Happen

9th November 2014

Last Thursday in Krav training I got my little finger dislocated on my left hand. There were both negative and positive aspects to this happening.

The Positives were:

1). My adrenalin was so high that it didn't hurt at all and I was able to laugh and joke about it, even joining the other guys for the final "Kida!" before I got driven to hospital.

2). It's my first bona fide "injury" in Krav and there's that adolescent part of my soul that regards it as a legitimate wound picked up in battle. I've been hurt before but tennis elbow and a compressed rotator cuff (shoulder injury) didn't really cut it.
3). I got to inhale the gas they use for local anesthetics when they fix stuff like this, meaning I got to be drunk without spending £25+ to get there.

4). My job is mainly outdoors and it's winter and tiddling with rain most of the time and I'm now on restricted duties at work meaning I'm indoors.

The Negatives however...

1). I have a P5 grading/ P Weekend coming up in four weeks so need to be fit for that. The injury means I will miss training and more importantly sparring training.

2). I missed Warzone 2: Behind Enemy Lines, a gun seminar that my club ran two days after I got injured. I'd been looking forward to this for about five weeks.

3). I'm on weird painkillers that make me feel shitty.

4). Most importantly, I've realised just how lousy my sparring is.

If we take point 4 from the Negatives.

I had hypnotherapy for my reluctance around sparring and/ or combat training and resolved some deeply horrible childhood issues that had led to this. Other side of this blackness though was the irony of actually not wanting to go as I didn't like it and to be honest just couldn't be arsed half the time. I took up Krav to stay fit and avoid fighting if necessary. Coldly touching gloves with someone then trying to kick and punch them for two minutes didn't seem to be very evasive. However I later learned that this is a fundamental part of Krav, especially from P3 and up as you will be beasted at a grading. We had about 30 minutes of full on sparring at my P4 test in March 2014. While I lasted the course, I lost a piece of a tooth, my gum shield and one contact lens.

I told myself I'd start to go in to the sparring again a few weeks before the P Weekend and get my stamina, cardio and skills up to speed. Problem was that this week I've finally seen that this is a part of training that you need to attend regularly.

One guy I was fighting was all over me, punching and kicking and even when we changed partners it seemed like a movie where the block is thrown the same time as the punch (basically because it's choreography and they know what's coming next). I was telegraphing most of my moves, dropping my guard and getting more and more knackered at time wore on. The clincher came when we were doing the final exercise (3 against 1) and I tried to block a stomp kick with my left hand. Something you are never supposed to do. I felt the 'thud!' and realised that I couldn't bend my little finger.

I stepped out to wrench off my soaking MMA mitt (to confused looks from my instructor) and saw it was now banana shaped.

Joking aside, this could have been a lot worse. The nurse at A&E (ironically his badge read "Nurse Practitioner") got me to inhale the nitrous oxide for a bit, then crunched the joint back into place. I will be sore for a bit and have limited mobility in my pinky, but I can go back pretty soon.

Bottom line is...you need to do something regularly to be good at it, not just when you feel like it.

## On The Bench

13th November 2014

After dislocating my left little finger by trying to stop a stomp kick with my hand I paid a visit to the fracture clinic...who signed me off for three weeks from active duties at work. This means I'm inside and not outdoors and am limited as to how much I can physically do. Awesome.

The yin to the yang is that I also can't train at Krav either.

Deciding to put a positive spin on this, I went along to the session last Tuesday, solely to watch the Sparring class.

I'd had suspicions that my sparring was lacking so thought half an hour sat watching, free from stress, fatigue or a boot in my groin would help me see just what I need to watch out for and improve upon.

As the main class filed out to go home, the four guys who'd elected to stay got kitted up in the bomb disposal vests and got going.

I was partnered with a big Polish guy the night I busted my finger and he was all over me, even knocking me down on the floor a couple of times. This time I watched him fight and he's a good fighter. He waits for you to come to him, which I picked up on last week, however what I hadn't spotted is that if you get too close he takes a couple of hits by protecting his face with his hands...and then follows up with a vicious hook to the side of your head.

As the group changed partners I watched the styles they fought in and a few things became apparent that I hadn't spotted before.

First of all, those that landed punches usually didn't telegraph their moves, something I do. Also, those that didn't get repeatedly walloped in the head had their hands up and their chins down, some things I fail to do regularly.

I had originally thought that the list of "wounds" picked up on the P4 grading last March sounded badass (lost contact lens, lost gum shield, chipped tooth) but now I realise it's because my guard was down and I wasn't striking properly. My kicking is weak, mainly due to lack of flexibility (Devil's Claw tablets from Holland & Barret and a few "Yoga for Dummies" You Tube videos are helping that) but also stamina and cardio training issues.

For one night it was beneficial to just sit and watch how other people fight, without the emotions and adrenalin (not to mention sweat) that come with being part of a class but not being able to see what's going on except for the guy facing you.

## Being HARD

15th November 2014

At the schools I attended as a child there was a sliding scale of being "hard".

That tiresome machismo that boys adopt after a certain age, became apparent to me when I was about 9. At my first Primary school there was no real posing or acting like a caricature of your favourite superhero. You simply did your thing and had your friends and just got on with it. We had our "top dogs" but they held that position through popularity amongst their peers. There was no need to pretend, as our playtimes were full of "pretend" anyway. Grease, Saturday Night Fever and the irritating TV show Happy Days were stupendously popular when I was a kid. One lunchtime the two most popular boys in my form, Ryan Perry and Jason Fitzmaurice (we didn't hang out with girls unless forced to...girls were smelly and stupid and into sissy things like skipping) got the rest of us together and gave themselves and us nicknames before we "got on our scrambling motorbikes".

Jason was the name giver and pointed to himself and went "Fonz" then to Ryan and went "Grease". These were the top names you could possibly have in an era of Richie Cunningham and Greased Lightning*** (which made us giggle as it had the words "shit" and "tit" in it...and was played on the radio a lot). Ryan acknowledged the given name with a smile and a nod, and Jason then named the rest of us.

I got to be "Spud".

Seriously, Spud?!!

We then pretended to be holding handlebars and ran up and down the playground making motorbike noises. This incident was notable for two reasons.

One, it was the only time I ever remember seeing all the boys in my class play a game together without teachers organising it. Two, I left as I thought it was boring and a few minutes later tried to come back but was told I couldn't. The club was closed to Spud now he'd resigned.

When I got to what was then called class M1, at 8 going on 9, I noticed that the 11 year olds were acting different to how we'd acted for so long. Now we were in the M section of school we got to use a different playground. One for older kids who got to wear their own clothes instead of uniform (if they wanted to, although the Headmistress was against it). A certain cockiness, surliness and adoption of superfluous gestures was adopted by them. Something that I picked up on very quickly was that the older kids didn't smile a lot. They were, it transpired, trying to look cool or "hard".

A catch phrase of the time was to say "Who let you

out?" if someone did something stupid or you just wanted to curtail an argument by putting them down. I once said this to a kid in my class who was friends with a surly, older boy who snapped back "I did, because he didn't belong in there."

Again, my over analytical brain was thinking that the original line about being "let out" was only an insult and not meant to be taken literally. That follow up didn't make sense.

Again, being older meant you had to be, or at least pretend to be "hard."

At Secondary school the regime was entrenched. Boys had to either be able to fight or put on a persona of "hardness" in order to avoid getting picked on or bullied.

If you came across as "hard" then you could call everyone's bluff until one of the genuinely hard kids offered you out.

So...ingrained in me and a lot of little boys as they grew up was that you had to be hard or, failing that, pretend your arse off in order to look like it.

Boys don't cry (a friend of my father once said how great it was when I pointed out that I hadn't cried in over a year), boys don't show too much emotion, boys can fight, boys like football, etc, etc.

Boys had to put on a facade of utter hardness and invulnerability to emotions that only puffs, fairies and girls reveled in.

Realising this wasn't in itself a revelation. What is eye opening however is just how much I carried this attitude with me into my adult life

The swagger when I walk. The poker face when I enter a crowded pub. The cold face when I'm stuck in traffic (countered by the "rage face" when I feel like having a go).

I, like many men believe I have to look "hard" even now. Old habits die hard, especially when they are so ingrained in us that we don't even know we're doing them. All that swagger and false bravado was nothing more than an attempt to put on a face that I fundamentally thought I had to wear.

In Krav Maga I've been told that the best way to defuse aggression is to avoid it. So, if you can walk away from a fight, then do it. If you are in a road rage incident then drive away or just don't lose your cool in the first place.

About six months ago a rude Scottish guy chased me up the street in his 4x4 because I'd stuck my finger up at him in traffic.

I looked in the rearview mirror to find him gesturing furiously for me to pull over and get out. So I did.

Not to be "hard" but because I was genuinely pissed off and angry. This burst his bubble and he simply sat in his car moaning about my lack of road etiquette but making no attempt to get out and confront me...like he'd been telling me he wanted to do.

He felt he had to look "hard"...along with millions of other guys.

The breakthrough in self perception has basically made me see that I don't have to hide my emotions or try and be tougher than I really am.

If you're a man, just think of the times when you've cried and felt ashamed for doing it. The only acceptable occasions for a blub are a close relative's funeral; at your children's birth or when watching footage of old men attending Armistice day on television. Society sets rules on just how much emotion we can feel as men, and tells us we have to fake as much as we're lacking.

To pretend is relatively easy. To be yourself is what's truly "hard".

## Krav Radar

19th November 2014

Today in Tesco I was at the self service tills when the security guard accompanied two Eastern European guys back into that area to clarify whether or not they'd paid for their groceries.

To set the scene, the self service area is semi enclosed, with the tills on two sides facing each other and a barrier at one end, with the exit at the other end.

There were about fifteen people in there, plus a couple of Tesco staff and it was pretty tight.

I first realised what was happening when I heard raised voices and the repeated phrase "I pay for it. I just don't have receipt!"

I turned around and the guard was standing well within personal space and BETWEEN both guys, trying to peer into the bag of one of them. I stood slightly back so I could see what was going on and one guy came up to me and tried to reach past me, saying "I used this till." As my shopping was in the area he was about to reach into, I stood in his way and asked "You alright?"

"Yeah, I uses this till for my shopping. You see receipt?"

There had been one as I'd turned up, and I'd taken it and put it on the side so it wouldn't be in the way. I reached for it myself as I was aware this guy was agitated, had possibly stolen something and I didn't want him near my stuff in case he tried to hide anything or worse, try to thieve any of my groceries too.

I handed the receipt to the security guard, but not the guy, who looked at it and said "This isn't for your stuff!"

They argued for a little while, and I watched them without turning my back in case it escalated and I had to back away or even try to help out. What was annoying me more than anything was that the guard had clearly NEVER BEEN TRAINED how to appropriately deal with this type of thing, as he had brought two potential shoplifters back to a crowded area filled with various people including an old lady and several women (and before anyone starts, they didn't look like women who could kick ass) plus a small child.

This didn't get any worse and the two men seemed merely annoyed that they were being accused. Neither swore or got angrier and they made no attempt to threaten the security guard who obviously thought he needed to solve the situation but had put other people (who had nothing to do with the situation), at potential risk by placing these guys and himself amongst bystanders. Worse, in a tightly packed area with limited movement and even fewer exit points.

The lads eventually simply walked off, ignoring the

guard, meaning his efforts had been not only inappropriately handled but for nothing.

While this was merely observation, I was pleased after that I'd attempted to assess it with the state of mind I'd been trained to in Krav Maga, which was to look at the potential threat and act (or not act) accordingly.

## P&G Camps
## Harlow Leisure Zone, Essex

5th December 2014

In late 2014, after being signed off sick for a month with a dislocated little finger I skipped down to the fracture clinic on Thursday the 4th of December, quietly confident of the doctor signing me on as "Fit For Work" and more importantly fit for Krav. Specifically, the annual P&G Weekend Training Camp being held in December. Master Zeev Cohen and Master Eyal Yanilov under one roof. Three days of top quality training from the highest ranked Masters in the world, finished off with my P5 grading.

The doctor however signed me off for a further 6 weeks and said with a stone face "Light technique training but absolutely no combat or sparring….and don't even think about the grading."

Drat!

I was also unable to get Friday off work.

Double Drat!!

So I decided to look at the positives and realised that two days of top quality training was better than none (but not as good as three) and while I would be unable to take the grading, it would be extra instruction in time for the next one in March 2015.

I got to Harlow Leisure Zone at about 8.15am on the Saturday to find people steadily drifting in. I grabbed a mega sized coffee and chatted to a guy from Bristol who said he been nervous at the start of Friday's training, but the whole thing was very well run. He added that there was lots of good technical stuff and it was all very well presented.

I'd had a few texts from friends who were there the day before, saying how tiring it yet fantastic it was and boasting of fantastic training drills they'd done during the day. As well as Zeev and Eyal there was also Moran Laskov in attendance, an E2 level and ex IDF Instructor, who had overseen my P2 test in 2013.

Instructors I recognised were amongst the arrivals, with Anna Surowiec from Active Krav Maga there. My own club's instructor Russell Brotherston was gearing up for G5. It was amusing to see what equipment people had brought with them. P levels had maybe a replica knife. Russell had a replica AK47 strapped to his backpack.

A husband and wife duo said, "Zeev works you hard but makes it a lot of fun." The husband had been in the Graduate side of the hall and said "The amount of knowledge passed on is incredible. You think you know a technique but it's a valuable experience."

At 9am as we stood in the main hall as Eyal addressed us and talked about the importance of learning Krav Maga properly and how the discipline required is a matter of mindset. After a warm up we did a technique involving stance and body language and how this can affect mood. This proved effective for me, as I was still sulking a bit about being signed off sick and not being able to properly join in. By the end of this I felt a lot more focused and positive and we then split into our respective zones. A dividing screen was drawn across the hall, separating the P levels from their bigger brothers and sisters on the G side.

We then formed up with Zeev Cohen and Moran Laskov. The initial part involved ground work with emphasis on the importance of bridging correctly when trying to tip an opponent or throw them off.

During a water break I spoke to one lady who said, "Zeev is amazing. I was quite intimidated by him at first but I've had problems with bridging for 2 years now and he sorted it within a few minutes."

This training proved to be good polish to skills I'd learned at previous levels. After moving through the various holds and releases we then had a knife chucked into the mix, meaning you had to block knife attacks with someone sitting on your chest. This was something I'd only touched on briefly before but again, it proved very useful.

As the guys moved to ground work and grappling I

had to step out and just watch. Observing this was beyond frustrating as I couldn't join in. Behind the curtain the G level students were making some serious noise and I wondered exactly what was going on in that mysterious "other" place.

After the grappling we switched to sticks, with Moran pointing out that we were doing our partners no favours at all by trying to be "nice" and not hit them hard. After people were still going relatively soft we then got told to pick up a strike shield and to throw three or four heavy blows to it, then drop the pad and attempt the stick disarm. This improved reflexes considerably as no one wanted to get whacked in the skull. One problem that repeatedly cropped up was people not assuming the correct posture with the stick defence, mainly due to the fact that you are looking down during a one handed, overhead stick disarm for the initial part of the technique.

Moran tried a method of getting us to "freeze" once we'd performed the initial block, and then get our partner to assess whether or not we had done it right. It was interesting to see just how much you miss through having to judge without sight, as both me and my partner were slightly wonky on the hand, fingers and arm positions, a fact which could prove dangerous or even lethal if whacked with a stick in a real life assault.

Some time later Jon Bullock approached us with a

filmmaker who was shooting a documentary about the P & G Weekend for future advertising. Jon got all 100+ of us to stand completely still and silent, with training knives and sticks, while facing each other and then introduced himself to the camera. At the words, "If you would like to know more, please check out the KMG website" we all went mental attacking each other, bludgeoning with sticks and knives, and hurling bodies around the hall. We only did two takes but it was a lot of fun and the note of humour helped alleviate much of the fatigue after going at it solidly for about 4 hours.

Later Eyal and Zeev switched sides and we had Eyal teach us. We were focusing on blocking kicks, with the main instruction being on how to prevent both long range and roundhouse kicks. After drilling this for quite a while, we moved on to going over the moves relevant for our prospective levels for some last minute rehearsals.

When the day's training ended we wiped the sweat away and sat with a creaking of joints in one big group while Jon Bullock gave us a pep talk about the upcoming Sunday grading. He repeated the earlier sentiments about not giving up and that, pass or fail, the experience would be useful.

He lamented people who would quit completely due to failing one grading and reminded us that we should look at every part of what we did as valid, and it was not just about getting the "cherry on top."

Afterwards I spoke to Eyal Yanilov.

"Everyone has put in 110%. Over the course of the weekend you can see skill improvement which makes it worthwhile. We have managed to make the P&G Weekend very good because we have dug deep into the curriculum. Of course the deeper we get, it's a trade off with how many things we cover. We try to work reasonably deep, from the material and the curriculum and reasonably wide. So we are dealing with a relatively wide range of subjects.

Also we did division for levels so when instructors were monitoring the participants they were divided according to the level they are going for. So in each level and each grade the participants were practicing what they felt was most necessary for them, with the monitoring from the instructors.

Naturally we also worked on the mental state with people to get them to change it. We worked on fighting spirit, courage, readiness all in order to create a better performance for self defence. Also the work you all did with posing, that changes the mental state."

He then left me with this quote to sum up the two days' training so far, "Change your attitude, change your posture, change your body language…and the attacker will change his mind."

Finally we all drifted away for a shower, a meal and some sleep before the big day.

\*\*\*\*\*\*\*\*\*\*\*\*\*\*\*\*\*\*\*\*\*\*\*\*\*\*

Sunday 07/12/14

Jon Bullock had warned us to be prompt for the grading day, as people needed to re-register before we kicked off. Nearly everyone looked nervous. A bloke going for P4 said, "It's a mixture of emotions. Anticipation, nerves and aiming to do the best I can."

Warming up on the side was a 69 year old practitioner. He was up for P2 and said, "I'm feeling good, plugging through. Confident but I'm not a good sparrer."

Behind that ever-mystifying curtain dividing the Ps from the Gs were some equally hyped people getting kitted up. I spoke to Anna Surowiec, Chief Instructor at Active Krav Maga. She was up for G5 and as she got ready she told me, "The training's been really good. Balanced with technical and physical aspects. I feel I've progressed, so for me it's about the journey."

After the formalities were out of the way Master Eyal called us over and spoke about the fact that to fail a grading was not something to get upset over, repeating and renewing what Jon had said the night before. He added that to pass or fail we should take away from the experience what we gained from it and not focus on the negative aspects. He told a tale of a man who'd done a test in Israel with Zeev Cohen, which was filmed.

Afterwards, the man said he remembered Zeev saying

"That was bad", "You did that wrong" and "That could be better" but the video showed him also being paid many compliments that he had blanked out, due to both stress and his mindset at the time.

Eyal then said that we cannot control an examiner or the decisions they make, only influence them and that they were like a priest in a confessional box or a surgeon in hospital. They did their job regardless of who was in front of them.

We then moved on to visualisation techniques. Eyal said to imagine the worst possible scenario we could such as getting divorced, losing a job, and being evicted all on the same day. Then to imagine the situation improving from that point on, in 6 or 7 steps. After we'd done this we stood up and visualised being attacked. The first time we would fall the ground without resistance. Then we would slowly add more to the scenario until we succeeded in overpowering and subduing our assailant before calling the police. This was designed to show us that the brain cares little for whether a scenario is real or imagined and by clearly imagining it we would be able to condition our minds to cope with the stress around such a situation.

After some stretching and about 10 minutes of light slow fighting (first time I've fought with one hand behind my back), the groups were split into their grading levels and I stepped out to get changed into my civvies. When I came back the curtain was drawn across the hall again with the grunting and hitting noises suggesting that the G levels were already going hard at it.

I briefly spoke to David Slade a senior instructor from Krav Maga Elite who was an examiner for the day. He said that this was the first time they'd had P&G together like this as previous events had been run separately.

He added that, "Having Zeev and Eyal in one room together is very special. Like an Abba reunion but less hairy."

Taking Eyal's advice to heart, I was determined to make the day as instructive as possible and not just sulk about being unable to participate any further. My club mate Graham was in the P5 chunk of the room and I'd spoken to him earlier about the weekend. He said that on the Friday they had learned from Eyal about dealing with the mentality of failure and coming back stronger.

Just before the gradings kicked off, my own club's instructor, Bartosz showed up to lend some moral support to our guys. Around the same time a guy from KMM also arrived to take G1. He was the first non-instructor Graduate level candidate from our club and it was good to know that people were now stepping into the higher ranks of Krav.

Examiner Moran Laskov gave me his opinions just before thing got underway.

"First of all I think the people here are very motivated and one of the things that I enjoy to see is people who are eager for knowledge. They have a lot of motivation, a lot of passion for Krav Maga and when you have passion, you can gain a lot of things like improve yourself. It doesn't matter if you are failing in a test, you have the passion, you like it. So I'm very happy to see that people are serious to train, even if it's hard to continue to train. I'm very please to see people asking questions and their character, they like to work."

The P levels were segregated into groups according to which patch they were aiming for. Shaun Weir and Stuart Hobbs from KMM were doing the initial moves for P2.

I was still jealous about not being able to participate but glad to see the enthusiasm that everyone was giving it.

The technical side of things was carried out with heaps of enthusiasm by everyone involved. From break falls, to choke hold releases to forward rolls, the assembled practitioners really gave it their all. Everyone had been warned there would be no lunch break so fleeting trips to the side of the hall to glug some water or an energy drink were common to see.

Around 2pm I stepped to the other side of the dividing curtain to take a look at what the G levels were doing. This was nothing like what I'd expected. While the Practitioners were working hard and giving it their all, the

Graduates were in another neighbourhood completely. Russell Brotherston was fighting, with 16oz gloves and a gum shield, along with Ana Surowiec and all the other G4 and G5 guys. A lot were instructors themselves. The fights were 1 vs. 1, one minute rounds of full contact, with nine rounds in total. Once they'd finished they then moved straight into 2 vs. 1. I have seen and done this myself before but what I witnessed left me open mouthed.

The guys were going full on, with Zeev invigilating and shouting encouragement or advice such as "Don't be gentle just because she's a woman, hit her!" or "The head is a legitimate target now, aim for the head!"

None had helmets on and during one melee a fighter caught a hammer punch to the side of his face from his opponent, his legs buckled and he sat down hard on the floor. Zeev simply requested someone else to jump in to take his place and encouraged the guy to get up. Another Graduate filled the gap but after less than thirty seconds he rose back up and joined in, giving it his all. This was impressive but what happened next was hard to believe.

Russell was one of the attackers fighting another G5 candidate At one point he clipped him in the chest and suddenly the guy dropped his left arm to guard his rib cage but carried on fighting with one fist, despite clearly being in a lot of pain. He saw the fight to the end but then collapsed, his face making it quite clear just how badly hurt he was. After getting some heat cream rubbed into it he carried on to the end of the grading, getting involved in several other fights plus weapon disarm scenarios. At the finish, he was heard remarking that every time he breathed in, his ribs hurt. Later we found out that he had a hairline fracture to one rib.

The best way to describe "going behind the curtain" was that it was similar to being at junior school aged 9 and, for the first time, being allowed to go up to Top Playground where the bigger boys and girls spent playtime. Different rules, different attitudes and different interactions. The G levels were tireless. None gave up, none backed down and that fighting had to be some of the most intense and skilled I've ever seen in Krav Maga.

Stepping back to the P side of the hall and the Practitioners were now going at it, with their sparring in full swing. Finally they stopped and as people got to their feet to grab a towel and gulp down some food I got a few minutes with Zeev Cohen.

"We've had an amazing weekend, from the aspect of how many people get to train which is an amazing number. It has grown since the last few years.

The professional level is extremely good and I'm very happy with how the level of Krav Maga is developing here in the UK. They are enthusiastic, have fighting spirit, the communication…it's quite amazing. It makes sense that if people train with us for years, and for long years then the requirement on their ability would go up and up. Technical, fighting spirit and skills. It's a different level of skills so you cannot compare someone in the P levels to higher level G. My motto for life would be 'Set your goal. Be determined. Get there."

As I turned around I saw every P student laying on their backs on the floor, stretching out and relaxing both mind and body, under Moran's instruction after the huge effort they'd put in.

The P groups then sat in relevant clusters around the hall while the treasured feedback was given and pointers to future performance handed over. David Slade was with P4 and P5 and I sat in to listen, mainly as the feedback was invaluable for my own future. The biggest problem on stick disarms was hand and arm position during the initial block while dropping guard during punches was another. It was good to see that nearly everyone passed, including those taking mock tests.

Some had come to the weekend with no intention of grading but instead to see how good their skills were, in a dummy run for a future exam and to get valuable advice. One woman had 75%, and was told that come an actual test she would undoubtedly do very well.

After feedback from Moran to everyone in the P side, that encompassed common mistakes and areas to work on, the certificates were given out. Then the group started to pack up and think about going home.

Back on the G side G4 and G5 were getting feedback from Zeev on the day but Gs 1 to 3 were still going at it with Eyal, at the far end. They didn't finish until after 6pm Russell passed, getting a grade of 92%.

The whole weekend was thoroughly enjoyable and an educational and instructive experience. The attitude and mental conditioning exercises that we did helped a lot of us and my "sickness", far from killing my desire to continue, has made me realise that sometimes you need to be patient to get what you want. Had I gone straight back in to the training and grading I might have injured myself worse, and been laid off for more than six weeks. By waiting, I'll be fighting fit for March and in the line with everyone else for the next time we grade.

Can't recommend this highly enough. A wonderful time had by all.

## 12 Days

### 17th December 2014

Last Friday we had the KMM Christmas night out. Nando's is always a favourite of mine, mainly because the local branch is 50 yards from my apartment, but also because there's something so very wonderful about lots of chicken based dishes smothered in chili sauce (not to mention the joys of the "bottomless coke").

Afterwards I said cheerio to the fifteen or so guys who were about to hit the town and made my way home. During the 90 second journey I saw a couple of young ladies I didn't know and noted that one had a nice ass. She then doubled over and violently puked all over the pavement...while her friend stood there laughing.

Christmas is a time when I like to relax, forget about Krav for a bit and just chill out. Usual stuff like huge boxes of chocolates at work, mince pies with a cup of tea and trying to avoid listening to any Cliff Richard Xmas songs on the radio. Christmas is after all, a time when we feel most able to relax. I don't mean that it isn't stressful because it certainly is. However when you "do" Christmas you aren't tuned in to danger. It's a time when the most we expect is to have a headache choosing and buying presents.

Seeing that woman power vomit all over Regent Street made me realise that the negative aspects of life get a little bit worse during this time, mainly due to the amount of alcohol people shove down their necks. Been there and done that, so I'm not judging BUT if there's one thing Krav has taught me (and in particular KMM's Chief Instructor Bartosz) it's that you need to be aware of what's around you.

I rarely use my mobile phone in the street, and if I do need to make/ receive a call or even change a song on the MP3 player, I will step into a space that is enclosed or semi-enclosed and look around me first.

Same at cash points, and same when getting into my car. I also lock the car as soon as I close the door\*\*. It's not that I'm paranoid, I simply regard these steps as common cautiousness on a par with locking my front door, checking the windows are closed and making sure I've turned off the taps before I leave my home every day.

Christmas is the time when people let their guard down. It's been statistically proven that most violent crime drops notably over Christmas week (exceptions being alcohol related crime and domestic violence) and we feel that this is a time to just be at ease.

A puking woman with a nice bum was an image that reminded me that life gets a tad silly over the festive period. Various scenarios could have sprung from that situation. Had she sprayed sick on a passerby, then there might have been a row. She might have needed help. She might have become aggressive with anyone who criticised her for honking up in public, or...., any number of things. Walking home from a Christmas meal with my Krav buddies I felt "safe" and in a good mood. I wasn't expecting danger or unpleasantness or seeing someone's alimentary canal go into spasms...because I assumed that the world was in as good a mood as I was.

What this showed me was that I need to keep my eyes open and remain aware of my surroundings, even as I look forward to turkey with all the trimmings.

I do Krav because it increases my confidence and allows me to walk in peace. Ultimately that means being aware of what's going on.

There's no magic shield like in the Ready Brek*** commercial to protect me against ne'er do wells. I walk in peace because I'm conscious of my surroundings.

This doesn't get to go on holiday.

---

*\*\* Soon as I turn the key, the door unlocks, meaning I have to lock it again or wait until I've driven 10 yards for it to self lock. Not a perfect world.*

*\*\*\* 1970s commercial on TV for a porridge breakfast cereal that said it was "central heating for kids".*

## Egone

### 21st December 2014

I am currently reading a very informative book entitled The Little Black Book of Violence by Lawrence Kane and Kris Wilder. It has the subtitle "What Every Young Man Needs to Know About Fighting."

This book was lent to me by a fellow practitioner at my club.

While perusing it last night, something struck a chord that is fundamental to the principles of Krav, but is sometimes oh so very easy to overlook in favour of the "sexy" bits of what we do.

A preface by Rory Miller (a police sergeant in the US when the book was published) states that he believe most people reading the book will simply cherry pick the parts they like. He goes on to say, "I don't think you can see past your own ego. I think that you will risk your own life and piss away good information to protect your daydreams."

Something that has occurred to me a lot lately is how violence is best stopped by anything other than violence.

I used to be a UK police officer and the experience was soul destroying in its stupidity, lack of basic common sense and political correctness over officer safety. We weren't trained to fight, only to subdue through holding and baton strikes absolutely COULD NOT be aimed at the head, regardless of what the Bad Guy might be coming at you with at the time. We spent 6 weeks on Race & Diversity training, but a measly 4 hours on use of baton and 1 hour on how to fire pepper spray (the only weapons 95% of UK cops carry on patrol).

Krav Maga to me is what the English police should be about. It teaches you to avoid conflict. That "FUCK OFF! STAY AWAY!" shouted at the top of your lungs is the best method to try first, if you have the distance and time. Krav talks about avoidance, de-escalation and getting the hell out of there if it can be achieved. It says violence is a secondary alternative that is played only when less confrontational options won't work.

But as we know, Krav also teaches us to be as brutal as possible, as quickly as possible with the minimum of effort and THEN get the hell out of there.

It's how the English police should be. Common sense and a lack of ego but able to be baddasses if the occasion demands it.

Problem is for me that it's very easy to get enticed by the funky side of Krav. We've all seen sparring sessions at our clubs where two good fighters go hammer and tongs on each other with grace and power. I personally imagine being whoever is the victor. Then there's the everyday interactions we see where we wonder exactly what we would have done had someone called us a "c**t" in traffic or pushed in front of us in a queue. I personally imagine them being humiliated, maybe even working in an Educational Block like Krav Vader, to make certain they keep their distance.

Problem is that my daydreams quite often cloud my judgment.

I don't like sparring cold bloodedly, although I'm not bad at it when I actually have a go. I can assess threat reasonably well and I'm not a coward. But all my badass fantasies, as I move further into Krav Maga and up the grades (currently P4).

Having seen movies where people simply pop dislocated joints back into place I never envisaged in a thousand years, having to be on restricted duties at work for nine weeks, repeated visits to the fracture clinic and a special splint being made at Warwick hospital after a dislocated pinky.

The least useful appendage on my entire body has affected my ability to train and means my cardio is so out of practice that I get out of breath running up the stairs.

Ego can be a killer. I've had it for most of my life and always imagined it to be a friend, mistaking it for confidence. Ego isn't confidence. Confidence is feeling that you are able to deal with what is in front of you. Ego is feeling that you can not only do it but do it perfectly and then have loads of women want to shag you because you're such an awesome badass.

It has taken 30 minutes of Yoga a day for over two months before I've become supple enough to kick higher than the belly button level of an opponent. My lack of flexibility was something I worked around until I became a teaching assistant at a Kiddy Krav class, and was having rings run round me by 6 year old girls (not to mention wincing as my back strained every time I bent down to pick something up during the sessions). I now have flexibility again, like I did in my 20s. But it's through adherence to a regime of stretching instructed by someone who knows more than me on the subject.

I see rude or threatening people in public a lot and 10 years ago I'd have jumped in to tell them to leave Mrs A or Mr B alone and be on their way

On some weird level I used to take all obnoxious behaviour as being somehow directed at me, if I was around when it happened. I think my logic was, "You know I'm here and are still doing this in front of me. Therefore you must think I'm a pansy who won't try and stop you."

Krav (plus a few other things, like getting dumped by my ex on a Skype call...just after she'd flown back to Europe on a flight I'd paid for) has helped me to mould and tailor my ego so I no longer feel that I'm a superhero

. When I'm drunk, all bets are off, but over this past year particularly I've got involved in things that have made me realise my own limitations and not to be ashamed of them but work with them.

Nick Maison and Jose Silva's Air Safety seminar was a sobering experience and as close to a hijack on a plane as I ever want to get. Forget being a hero, you are lucky if you can even see straight as the "terrorists" shove you around, order you not to look at them and do their best to disorientate you. Nick even said before we started, "If any of you feel like taking on any of the hijackers then feel free...but we WILL give you a kicking and then throw you off the plane"**

Having met both Eyal Yanilov and Zeev Cohen they are both softly spoken and humble men who appear without ego BUT are badasses. After the second day of P Weekend in December I was in reception at Harlow Leisure Zone when they both left for the evening. They did not stand out at all, did not swagger and would have blended into any crowd.

Ego can be dangerous. It ties me into adolescent fantasies about vanquishing the evil hordes and being the bully hunter I always wanted to be. It's only be accepting the drab reality of my own limitations that I can now build upon that and walk through life in a way that means I will assess situations logically and with my mind, not my ego.

Egone.

----------------------------------------

\** *Actually a decommissioned 747 on the runway of Bournemouth airport. We weren't airborne.*

## The Shovel or The Paintbrush

30th December 2014

Many years ago when I was a little boy, I was sat in class listening to Mrs Drakeford telling us about archaeologists (thank Christ she never put that word in our weekly spelling test) and she asked us offhandedly if we knew what they used to dig up dinosaur skeletons. After much humming and hahhing and being told that spades, shovels, forks and JCB diggers were not the answer she then wrote on the blackboard.

"Paint brushes."

We all scratched our heads and made surprised noises for a couple of minutes, unable to grasp in our little brains how a tool we used to paint pictures with every Tuesday afternoon, could possibly be used to dig up a Stegisouraradasous or a Triangelerotops.

She patiently explained that an archeologist couldn't get a spade and "just go dig, dig, dig!" but would instead have to patiently rub away with gentle bristles, the dirt and detritus covering what they wanted to unearth. When we pointed out this could take weeks Mrs Drakeford said, "It takes YEARS."

I've been doing Krav for about 3 years now and something I've learned is that it's very easy to reach for a shovel when a paintbrush is sometimes required.

When I took P3 in October 2013 I remember Jon Bullock, head of KMG UK saying to us, with examiner Rune Lind stood by his side, that it was from this point forward "no longer about collecting patches." We had a much harder journey ahead of us and blindly or short sightedly charging forward to grasp the next grade's memorabilia was something that wasn't going to happen.

Anyone who's taken P3, 4, 5 and up will know just how different they are from P1 and P2.

A paintbrush is a useful tool when aiming for higher grades as the shovel you are handed at your grading is good only for 6 months until your pride calls you to take the NEXT grading. I know for a fact that I cut corners and try to cram in as much as I can as late as possible, hoping that rolls will be cut for time (or lack of mats) and that I'll get the much coveted "group of 3" like I did on P2, so that there is less attention on me and more time to take a breath and watch how my partners do the techniques.

My "shovel" is that I don't go about my planning, training, and technique revision with patience, attention to detail and a desire to get it all "just right" but that I bludgeon my training, trying to get the most difficult moves done to satisfaction and hope the other candidates are huge in number on the actual day.

I remember feeling at my P4 grading that, had I failed, I

probably wouldn't come back any more. The week before I'd been nervous beyond endurance and my fingernails were bitten to little bloody stumps. I wasn't doing this as a sulk or a protest but simply because I didn't want to feel that bad again.

Not a noble, warrior-esque emotion to hold and one I'm most certainly not proud of...but it was there and I acknowledge it.

Overall, a paintbrush is a better tool when preparing for a grading. Take my time, relax and go over the moves at home in front of the DVD appropriate to my level. Learn for at least two months before I go, the moves specific to my upcoming grade and go in with the knowledge that I have drilled things as well as I possibly could. Had I used a paintbrush for P4 I would have felt more confident and loose.

Not ice box levels of coolness, but enough so I was sure that even with an Israeli E level examiner's eyes boring into me as he hovered with a clipboard, I would be able to give it my best, and not simply "hope" that it all came together.

Some things take time.

## The Butterfly Collection

4th January 2014

On the wall in my dining room I've got my P4 certificate in a picture frame. In the corners are my patches for P1, 2 and 3. When I pass P5 the 4th patch will join the others and when I get G1 I'll start a new frame next to the existing one.

Until tonight however, I had all four patches in that frame. I never wore my patches, they went straight into that frame, like captured butterflies, forever preserved in their glory and for me to gaze proudly at over breakfast coffee and cereal before I headed out to work.

I told myself this was due to not wanting to spend time every six months sewing the patch on and that for me it was enough to have passed and I didn't feel the need to advertise my grade.

Truth was a little different.

To me those patches were rare, much sought after and had been achieved through nerves, training, more nerves and the milling that is an actual grading. I had to do P4 twice due to a conditional pass in the March 2014 test (I had passed with 73% but like a prospect in a biker gang, I couldn't get the "top rocker" until I'd gone that extra mile, in this case doing stick defences again, back at my own club).

The patches were like exhibits in a private museum. Something so precious that I was afraid that I'd lose them forever if I didn't treat them with reverence and respect. I didn't put them on my Krav pants because to me they were to be worshipped. Delicate things that I was so very lucky to have.

On some level I think I was afraid to lose them and feared that this exchange might happen in training one night.

"Excuse me, your patch says you're P4. Can you just show me forward to backward roll please?"

"Errrr....."

The higher I rose through the Practitioner ranks, the more I felt like I had to "be" something more than I was comfortable being. I had fought so hard to get those patches that I kept them behind glass on a wall in my house, so I knew where they were and could rest assured that they were safe.

Yesterday I bought some iron on Velcro strips and tonight I ironed them on both the P4 patch and both pairs of training trousers. Tomorrow I will train with the patch on my leg for the first time.

Sometimes it's harder to feel comfortable to have achieved something, than it is to actually achieve it.

## Krav Maga Midlands- P1 Grading
## Stratford upon Avon High School

January 24th 2015

Krav Maga Midlands' first in house grading since 2010 (not counting the "technical pass" retests from last year) was something we'd all been expecting and the actual students going for it, were nervous about.

KMG had handed over the responsibility for Practitioner 1 gradings to individual clubs. Only P2 and up would now be graded at national events.

I spoke to one lady on Thursday in training about the upcoming test and she said "I'm really nervous but I do know it and I'm hoping I don't freeze on the day."

Another said, " Looking forward to tomorrow, nervous excitement I guess. Hope it goes ok, but the ground work and break-falls are a concern for a bigger guy like myself."

Bartosz, our Chief Instructor said, "I'm looking forward to it, we'll see what's going to happen. We'll assess our students and give them good feedback at the end."

Me and a few of the other guys had decided to go along and support those taking the exam. I remember well the nerves, anxiety and sense of bewilderment about my first grading, back in October 2012.

While I'm nervous at ALL gradings (P4 being the one

that pushed it into the stratosphere) there's something uniquely nerve wracking about the Practitioner 1 test. You don't know what to expect; most people have no idea what's going to happen; and it is quite possibly the first time you've been assessed on your physical skills, be it in Krav or any other type of situation.

I got to Stratford upon Avon High School at 12.15pm and the guys were waiting in the foyer near the sports hall. A lot of worried faces and I spoke again to the same lady who assured me she wasn't feeling nervous now. Her 8 year old daughter who attends Junior Safe Krav Maga on a Monday in Leamington Spa, looked up from her colouring book and went "Yes you are." That got a laugh and I also spoke to someone who told me, "Just looking forward to getting started and getting into it to be honest. I'm trying to think of it as a training session."

Another said, "I'm feeling incredibly nervous but I'm looking forward to it and I'm going to enjoy it."

Quite a few guys had turned up to cheer on their mates. The test was conducted by Bartosz and Russell Brotherston. As the students lined up Bartosz reassured them that while they were obviously nervous as it was a new experience for them, they should give it their all and do their best. They then launched into the warm up for a while and after working up a sweat were split into pairs. With eleven guys taking the test, there was one group of three. They all started on some striking moves and then switched to straight punches.

As the hours wore on, you could see the Krav maps appearing on people's T-shirts as the sweat flowed. Everyone was giving it their all and it was great to see how no one flagged in their energy levels and each one was going full out to perform 100% their best.

Russell and Bartosz walked around and between the fighting pairs (and the 3), making notes and occasionally conferring. After three hours they then moved to forward rolls with mats being laid out in a line. From personal experience I know how difficult it is to get this right.

It took me about a week to crack it for my P2 exam and again the guys performed it well.

They then paired off again and went for some striking and kicking work before rounding it all off with 50 push ups, 50 sit ups and 50 squats, getting a final good sweat on before we moved into a smaller sports hall. Bartosz told everyone to get a drink and a bite to eat, while he went into a private room with Russell to compare notes.

After about 15 minutes they came back and the students sat on the floor around them while they talked through the common mistakes made (knife defences being high on the list) and demonstrated the correct way to perform the moves. This is something I've seen at every grading I've taken and is invaluable feedback.

Finally they moved on to the grades and called names out. Individual feedback was given and everyone had passed. We applauded and finally everyone got to get up and think about going home. The lady I'd spoken to was grinning broadly, clearly happy to have passed. Her husband from the Leamington Spa class, and her two little daughters were very proud for her. She told me..."Really, really awesome. Really, really good. Really enjoyed it."

Russell said, "I'm pleased with how they all performed. There's always things that need to be fixed. That's always there, I mean I get that when I grade (laughs). Aggression was good, determination was good."

Another student said, "I'm pretty confident. Really enjoyed it, it certainly gets the blood pumping. I feel like I'm on the start of a very long journey. It's a big mountain to climb."

One guy was clearly over the moon and said "I'm really happy, hopefully be going for P2 in October now."

I got a quick word with Bartosz who said, "Good, just a couple of things to work on like knife defences and 360s. Very good footwork and pressure drills."

A fab day and it was fun to be there to offer support as it felt very much like a family affair with friends backing one another up and shouting encouragement when needed.

## Step 5

3rd February 2015

Yesterday something finally came into view that has been hovering on the horizon like a shy teenage boy on his crush's doorstep, with a bunch of flowers on Valentine's Day.

Of all the things that I thought would help me see where I was being held back in my life, I never once imagined it would be a reunited 1980s boyband.

I was bored and flicking through channels on You Tube and for some reason one of the links in the right hand menu was "Jon Knight sings step 5". This referred to the reunited New Kids on the Block at a live gig about 5 years ago and the bit of the song "Step By Step" where each member of the band sings a "step". Danny is 1, Donnie 2, Jordan 3, Joey 4 and Jon 5.

I was mildly curious as to why this was so noteworthy as to warrant a video of its own. After all, Jon's line is simply "Don't you know that the time has arrived?" I asked myself if NKOTB fans were so sad as to post a video that highlighted one bit of one song sung by one member of a quintet. Then I watched it and it became more puzzling. Once Jon sings the line the other guys jump on him like he's a striker in a World Cup soccer final who's just scored a goal. They hug him and are clearly over the moon and Jon is grinning and very happy. Checking out the comments section it turned out that this was the first time ever that Jon had sung that line at a live concert. Every other gig (and remember, that song came out in 1990 when the band were at their peak) the line was sung by Joey.

So, what is this to do with Krav? Well, I looked a little deeper into this and it turned out that Jon Knight was the reason that the New Kids split up in 1994. He left the group so they decided to call it a day. I remember them splitting up because back then they were the biggest band around. Bigger than One Direction or N 'Sync and rivaled only by The Backstreet Boys in later years (who they went on tour with recently).

But I digress....

In the late 80s and early 90s Jon Knight had the world at his feet. A multi millionaire by the age of about 21 he was loved by millions of screaming, adolescent girls and had his picture everywhere. From 1990 to 1991 the New Kids on the Block made ONE BILLION dollars on worldwide merchandise and netted about 25 million US dollars EACH in that same tax year. What more could a young man possibly want?

Once he quit the group he went into real estate and was out of the public eye almost completely, living on a farm and being reclusive.

It turned out that he was plagued by panic attacks and anxiety and hated being in public. The pressure and stress he felt was something he covered up as best he could. He was the "shy" one of the group and was quiet in interviews. He went on Oprah in 2001 to talk about how he felt and looked like a guy waiting for a reprieve on death row. Shaking, sweaty and almost in tears he told Oprah that he felt relaxed to which she replied "This is you relaxed?" He was clearly in immense discomfort but dealing with it as best he could. He said that once he left the band in 1994 he spent about the next three years sleeping and trying not to think too much. Emotionally he was a wreck.

Not due to the pressures of stardom, but because something within him was hard wired to hate the sight of crowds. He said that he felt he was going to die and that the adrenalin you would usually associate with a sudden scare, was with him all the time, every day.

The face he put on for the public back when the New Kids were actually kids, was a facade. I've no doubt he had pressure put on him by the people funding the cash cow that was NKOTB, who probably couldn't give a shit about his issues. However he masked it as best he could and it ate away at him until something snapped and a guy of 23 years of age, with millions in the bank, simply rolled over and went to bed for three years.

That video of him singing step 5 at the age of 42 was for him a personal milestone and the other guys in the group knew that.

I have been a walking anxiety attack for much of my adult life. My tenure in the UK police was cut short by bullying but the people who did that to me had identified what they perceived as weaknesses and flaws in someone entitled to arrest other people. I lacked mental stamina and was prone to empathy. Problem was that they used underhanded and unpleasant methods to get rid of me. I have both Enhanced Emotional Memory AND a very vindictive streak which can be activated if I'm mistreated.

When things go wrong my fear builds and builds until I'm creating monsters in my head. I find sleeping to be a warm and safe retreat from the horrors of life.

My father lives in the gorgeous holiday village of Plakias in Crete, Greece. He retired out there in about 1997 and the place is beyond wonderful. Blue seas, fresh fish restaurants, scuba diving, cliff jumping, cold beers, the list goes on.

The first summer I spent there in 2008, I had just left the police and spent most of my time drinking myself into oblivion. I would sleep for ridiculous amounts of time, the record being 36 hours in bed with a hangover that became self pity that became a desire to simply give up. Being that pathetic, felt normal and safe and the most sensible thing to do with how bad I felt.

I've never been able to simply kick back and enjoy things for the anxiety that eats away at me.

I do Krav Maga and I'm now a P4. Tonight my E1 instructor complimented me personally on my performance in class with a smile and the words "You did a good job today." I'm still floating on that but with Krav I don't enjoy myself as much as I pretend to.

I don't like sparring, a subject I've covered on here before. I get nervous just going to class and although this has dissipated over time, that prolonged Jon Knight-esque panic attack is still there. My biggest worry is that my instructor will call me out to demonstrate a move or succession of moves or a technique. I fear not understanding his instructions or that I'll get knocked on my arse or that I'll look like a dick but most of all that everyone else will be looking at me. Like Jon said in his Oprah interview. I'd just rather go home. The stress is phenomenal.

It's not rational or proportionate but it's there. Anxiety about being in public and being the focus of attention. I saw Jon Knight on Oprah from that 14 year old recording and it struck a chord. A guy who had wealth beyond imagining and was famous beyond belief was unhappy with his lot because of a psychological condition that he couldn't override without help.

Quite often people will say things like "Snap out of it" or "Don't be so ungrateful" or "How can you NOT enjoy this?" Thing is, if you don't then you don't and that's just how you are. Singing to millions of teenage girls and having your face on hundreds of different items of merchandise will not please you no matter how much you tell yourself that it should.

My P4 grading was far from a pleasant experience. My imagination was running riot and my stress levels were through the roof. I didn't enjoy the grading and the closest I came to actually having a good time was when I was so tired that my anxiety faded into the nether of my exhaustion and I just had to focus on the job at hand. As it was I got a conditional pass and did better than the 20 or so guys who failed the test.

Similarly, I feel I should pretend to enjoy fighting. That I should be comfortable in the four bar patch and show an aura of calm and power proportionate to my level (right now I'm the highest level student regularly attending the venues I go to). I don't feel comfortable in a lot of things and I've pretended for a very long time that I am.

The equivalent for me of singing step 5 would be to choose to fight a guy bigger than me who I know is a more skilled fighter and do it because I WANTED TO and not just to prove I'm not a pansy who fluked all his gradings.

Anxiety can be a killer of progress. Honesty can thwart it.

## Just One

### 8th February 2015

Yesterday I went to the gym and rejoined it. Cost me over £50 for a month's usage (cheaper if you sign up for six months in one go, but I like to Not Be Tied Down) but I thought it an investment wisely laid, mainly as I have my P5 grading in a few weeks.

P5.

A grade that once seemed as distant as my 30th birthday; the end of my school days; or my grandmother not being around. A grade that I believed was only held by badass beefcakes or people gearing up to be instructors at the next G camp.

P5.

Something I know I need to be fit for so I can take the 30+ minutes of full on sparring at the end of the technique based stuff. Something I know I have to devote the next six weeks to getting right by practicing in front of the TV (the joys of a HDMI cable and a laptop) and attending class at least twice a week.

But...

I also need to boost my cardio and that was an issue I sorted out yesterday. The gym I use has a very friendly guy in there who appears to regard working out and training with the same passion that I reserve for breathing. He recommended the "300 Workout" which I initially thought was based upon pre-historic Spartans in codpieces but turned out was 300 reps, on 5 or 6 machines in as fast a time as you can do.

The workout took about twenty minutes but felt like over an hour.

However it was exactly what I needed and while I didn't do it today (as my body felt like someone had been at it with a steak tenderiser) I'm going to do my damnedest to avoid the trap of missing "just one" session in the run up.

My desired regime is yoga at least three times a week, cardio 3 times and Krav twice. Plus doing dry runs from the P5 DVD my instructor gave me, about three or four times a week. The sparring on P4 was no harder than the sessions we do at the club, but with the adrenalin and nerves and all the other stress it felt like hell on earth. It was only when I saw the G4s and 5s going at it last December under the eyes of Zeev Cohen that I realised what I'd done was mere prep.

But I digress...

Missing a session through my desire to sup a couple of pints of Guinness; play "Call of Duty: World At War- Nazi Zombies"...again; read a book; watch episode 6 of TV show Banshee...or any of a list of excuses is something that could not only bugger up my chances of passing but actually cause me to get injured AGAIN like I have in the past when I let things slide through laziness or not adhering to some semblance of discipline over my training.

There is something rock 'n' roll about feeling fit enough to just keep going when those around you are grasping their knees and dry heaving. Feeling that you know the moves and can give it your all without wondering if you are just fluking it. Knowing that you are fitter than guys half your age.

Just one time out can become two, then three. And then I'm stuck on 4.

## The Other Sort of Brave

18th February 2015

On a Monday night I help out at a Kiddy Krav Maga club called Junior Safe Krav Maga.

That isn't a pint sized version of Big Krav, it is in fact a specially tailored set of activities for young children.

We focus on anti-abduction techniques, team work, anti-bullying and overall me and the instructor Russell doing our best to get the kids to go into full attack mode, if we pick them up or grab them.

At the end of the class (which lasts about 50 minutes) we line them up kneeling on the mat facing us and we choose two children who have shown the most enthusiasm, team spirit, courage and determination. Russ chooses one and I choose the other, and we have a quick chat to make sure we're not picking the same kid and to go over the reasons for the selection. They get the coveted places next to us, (one by him, one by me) and we tell them and the other kids what they did to deserve that 'honour'. We then bow and shout "Kida!" and hit the mat with our fists and everyone claps before we go home.

Last week we had a handful of new kids starting. One lad was about 6 years old and very small. He was clearly having the time of his life, running around and grinning from ear to ear. During a game where me and Russ try to pick the kids up they have to lay into us as hard as they can or we won't put them down again, this lad had no fear of two tall men in sparring helmets and MMA mitts trying to repeatedly grab him and was laughing and smiling the whole way through.

He got a position at the end of class. I chose him and specifically stated that it was because he was so brave and gung ho and that, on his first lesson, he was super confident and I admired his courage.

Russell's selection was someone I had been going to choose myself. She was the other sort of brave. A very small 5 year old girl who had, for a few weeks, sat on the sides with her mum and watched the other children running around, dodging me and Russell. She was clearly scared and overawed by it all and her eyes were like saucers as she saw us hurling foam pads around, putting kids over our shoulders and making a lot of noise. Attempts to coax her into joining in were met with a mute shake of her head and when she did eventually join in an activity she quickly left again in tears. It was too much for her. All these big people making a lot of racket and knocking each other around. She was smaller than the smallest kid in the class (who also happened to be her friend) and it was very clear just how frightened she was.

This week she joined in and stayed for nearly all of the

class. At the end we played a game where the kids were in two teams and had to run past me and Russell, and if stopped had to lash out with kicks and punches to make us let go if we grabbed them. Both of us were padded up with the helmets on and this little girl was on the team I was facing. I could see the terror in her face that meant she probably wouldn't do it so suggested that her friend ran with her. This proved to be the key to it all, as she then felt safe enough to join in with both of them booting me in the groin and punching me as I tried to hold her.

She got the second place next to Russell at the end before the final Kida, because as Russell said to everyone, she was scared yet carried on. The other sort of brave.

After the class I spoke to her in the corridor and she still looked a bit scared. I crouched down in front of her and said, "I'm very proud of you. It's very difficult to be brave when you're frightened and you did that. Give me a high five." She did, and smiled and then her mother asked me how she could stop a bigger girl at school who was pulling her hair in the playground. Me and Russ demonstrated the technique and when I got her to do it she punched me as hard as she could. We all laughed and noted that the next time that older girl bullies her, will probably be the last one.

It's things like this that make doing this completely worthwhile.

## Unique Practitioners- Goz Gozwell

22nd February 2015

*Goz Gozwell is a Krav Maga practitioner with KMM, practicing at the Solihull and King's Heath branches of the club. She also works in an all male prison.*

**"So how long have you been a member of Krav Maga Midlands?"**

"Since a year last November."

**"What do you do for a living?"**

"I work in the prison service. I'm custodial manager rank, which is the equivalent of an Inspector in the English police. I line manage 25 prison guards directly and I work in the security and intelligence department so I also run the gaol on a rota basis. The prison has over 1000 category B and C prisoners, so I have to run a prison with that many people."

**"Do you ever have to go hands on with the prisoners? To be in actual physical contact with them?"**

"Yes, you do. We're trained in control and restraint which are techniques we have to refresh every year. The aim now is also on de-escalation techniques rather than going hands on but even putting a "hand on" as in putting a hand on someone to make them move is classed as physical contact and we have to fill out paperwork to justify it. At my rank I normally turn up at the end and oversee the incident and assess what's going on."

**"Just to set the scene for those reading this, how tall are you?"**

"I like to kid myself I'm 5 feet 4, but I'm really five two if I'm lucky."

**"What category prisoners do you deal with?"**

"We take all sorts. Some times we get uncategorised prisoners and they get cat A. That's the highest security prisoner you can get. Highest risk to the public. As a rule we're category B which is one down from maximum security. We have remand, sentenced, lifers. We have cat D who return because they fail their open conditions. We can have every type of prisoner. It's a very mixed population."

**"With over 1000 prisoners, how many guards work in the prison on a shift?"**

"Well, the unit I used to run holds 200 prisoners and you'd normally work an SO, Senior Officer, and five. Quite often when I was a prison officer you'd get me on a spur which is half of a landing and there'd be me to about 60 which is quite average."

**"Have you had any physical attacks or altercations with prisoners?"**

"Yeah, I mean I've been lucky I've been in the job 12

years but I've been involved in control and restraint of prisoners. I've had prisoners square up to me. In my job, unlike in Krav, I try to use a lot of de-escalation. Sometimes you're on your own when the altercation occurs. So, over the years I've been involved in all sorts."

**"Do you carry batons?"**

"Yes we do. We carry the big extendable batons which are similar to the police. We don't have any CS or gas, or any stab vests or anything like that. Now the population has changed there's a lot of hand made weapons on the units, a lot of drug use so we're dealing with the same people that the police are outside but without the equipment. That's why we do have to rely on de-escalation. Also we work in closed spaces so if you're in a cell you wouldn't be able to use gas anyway. Pepper spray is used very rarely if the National Tactical Group are called in, if we have a situation that we can't deal with locally. I've been involved in hostage situation where three prisoners are in a cell or behind a barricade and we have had to use pava."

**"Why did you take up Krav?"**

"I always wanted to do a martial art but I didn't know what. For about 10 years I've been talking about it. It was originally nothing to do with the job. I'm a bit of a rough and tumble person, although contrary to belief I'm not actually a very aggressive person. I don't like fighting.

So it's for my own personal fitness, my own personal protection but also it has changed the way I look at things at work now. So if I was on my own I wouldn't think twice to use Krav now rather than control and restraint because you can't do it with a group of people so it's more practical which is why I like it. In a cell no situation is the same. You've got bunk beds, you've got furniture, maybe weapons all sorts. It's all risk assessed but spontaneous stuff isn't, you just react."

**"So has Krav helped you at work?"**

"I'm more conscious now of people behind me when I'm on walkways for example. I move and scan more. When we did our last control and restraint refresher, which we do yearly, I realised just how much more practical Krav is. I work with a lot of female officers in a male prison. So the obvious thing is to disable a threat quickly. If I was on my own and I felt threatened I would use Krav now."

**"The motto is 'So that one may walk in peace' after all"**

"Yes, it's down to perception. My colleagues and even the prisoners now think I can take care of myself.

It's part of it, how you carry yourself. It's about perception and someone backing off and leaving you alone."

**"You have all male prisoners. How many of the staff**

**are female?"**

"There's a lot more now but it's still very male orientated. It used to be a job that people went into from the army. That's changed now, it's more about people skills. I also find that in a male prison, women tend to keep the peace better. As a rule prisoners are more respectful of females. When you're like me you can be an authority or mother figure. Some of them have never had the word 'no' said to them before and they've got no boundaries so you're having to almost parent some of the prisoners."

**"That's interesting because I would have imagined it would be a lot of wolf whistling."**

"You do get that as well. You get a lot of inappropriate behaviour and you have to obviously stamp that out and challenge it because if you don't you know that there'll play on that. They know that I'm not somebody who's easily intimidated."

**"Do you think that Krav Maga should be taught to new people coming into the prison service?"**

"Yes, I do. It's a lot more practical. Apart from control and restraint we also do breakaway and personal protection. For the staff and civilians it would be so much more practical. Even if it was just to shout "GET BACK!" with a knee or a kick. It's very practical and that's what I like about Krav."

**"Why do you think this country has such a 'softly, softly' approach to use of force, both in the police and the prison service?"**

"In this job there will always be staff who take it too far and they can almost be barbaric. They use excessive force when they don't need to and because of things that have happened in the past such as prisoners who've gone on to commit suicide or control and restraint that's gone wrong. I think that's why it changed. People can asphyxiate if they're in the wrong position. Every year our syllabus gets changed. There's techniques they take out because they're considered indecent. It's a fine line. Also there's a lot of paperwork now."

**"Finally, what would your motto for life be?"**

"Feel the fear, do it anyway. Push past it. I'm six feet tall in my head."

**Acting Up**

1st March 2015

Assisting at Kiddy Krav Maga classes is LOADS of fun. At Junior Safe Krav Maga every Monday in Leamington Spa I get to run around the mat for nearly an hour with anything between 8 and 15 children aged from 5 to 11 and play loads of games with them.

Fundamentally we are teaching them to defend themselves against Bad People, so as a bonus I get to be a movie villain like the Sheriff of Nottingham from Robin Hood or Vector from Despicable Me. We pick them up, grab them and bop them on the head with spongey pads. All to improve their reflexes, boost their confidence and above all make it much harder in real life for a genuine Bad Person to make their lives difficult.

We play team games; games based on endurance; games based on single minded determination and at the end we choose two students who have shone out and they get to kneel next to me and the instructor Russell for the final bow.

This shows the rewards this kind of thing holds for me but last week it went a step further when Russell's car broke down.

He cancelled the class and apologised to the parents via

text and Facebook. I called him up and was like "Err... I can carry this today if you want. Why didn't you ask?"

Ever the gentleman, he replied "I didn't want to simply assume you'd do it."

At 3 hours notice I was a tad nervous and as Russell reversed his decision to postpone the class I made mental notes on what games to play with the kids.

That annoying inner gremlin was whispering in my ear saying such unhelpful things as "What if they don't want to work with you. Russell is their favourite, not you?" Or "What if you can't control them and they start acting up and won't listen to you?"

I told the voice to do one, and carried on planning the lesson.

When I got there the kids were drifting in, clearly hyped that they still had a class and running about as normal. I was expecting about 5 of them but by the time I got them lined up for the first "Kida!" there were 12.

Eep!

I explained that Russell was unable to make it but we'd still have loads of fun. As the usual toys were locked in Russell's car which was now at the mechanic's shop I had brought a pillow from home and chucked that at them for a bit. If caught they had to do a handstand against the wall and could only be "released" if someone crawled under them. After a few push up and sit ups we then moved on to team work with me padded up (groin guard being a pre-requisite when working with little people who are being taught to kick) and wearing a helmet. I got them to run at me in pairs and I would grab one of them. They had to work together to get that person free. One or two missed the point and hurtled off to the end of the room while their mate struggled.

"Great friend you are!" I would shout until they then ran back and dished out a few kicks and punches to make me let go.

The parents sitting round the edge of the room had offered to help out if I needed it so I had one of the dads try and flip me over while I tried to remain belly down on the floor. Kids got into that one and we worked out a few of their favourite games such as Zombie Tig (harder to understand than American Football) and Dodge Ball.

Finally I got a ringside mother to "volunteer" to help me with the last game of the session. The kids were in teams and had to run up one at a time (apart from one little girl who ran with her best friend) punch the strike shields we were holding and then push us to the back of the room and run back to their mates.

Ever competitive they were cheering each other on until the last one came through.

After the final bow I felt both relieved that the lesson had gone well and also elated as it was LOADS of fun. A few of the parents thanked me, with one or two paying compliments and I got some of the kids to beat me up for a souvenir video.

Brilliant time.

## How I Looked Vs. How I Felt

8th March 2015

In June of last year me and 9 others were personally chosen by Eyal Yanilov to fight the Predators at the KMG World Tour. The Fast Defence guys from Wayne Hubball's Adrenaline organisation.

I've blogged about this before but something I haven't really touched upon is how different the experience looked compared to how I felt about it.

I'm currently reading Geoff Thompson's book "Fear: The Friend of Exceptional People." It's a tremendous book, crammed with awesome advice about how to cope with being scared. His best advice is simply to say "I can handle it, whatever it is."

He points out that fear is felt by everyone to some degree and if anyone says they have never been frightened then they are lying. Fear is necessary to function in life. As the saying goes "Fear shows you where the edge is." But the problems arise when fear is not acted upon but suppressed or pushed aside or ignored. Then it stays around like the smell in a bachelor pad bathroom the morning after a stag do. It helps no one and is only destructive.

Last June there were over 100 of us, eager eyed

practitioners sat on the floor at Hengrove Leisure centre in Bristol, UK. Eyal Yanilov was there and it was enough to make me nervous just being in the same room as this guy. As embarrassing as that is to admit, it was how I felt. There is after all, a difference between how we feel and how we think we SHOULD feel. Jon Bullock the head of KMG UK was also there along with a vast array of UK instructors.

As the initial introductions got underway, without warning two uncouth, obnoxious blokes appeared in the seating area to one side and shouted (amongst other things) that we were all a bunch of "fucking wankers" and Krav was a "load of shit." When Jon Bullock approached them to tell them to leave, one threw the drink he was holding at him. The guys looked for all the world like two ex soldiers or unemployed oil rig workers who had had too much to drink and felt like taking on a room full of Krav Maga students and their teachers, just for kicks. After nervous laughter the seminar resumed, only for the two guys to reappear at the other end of the room in Predator outfits. Alan Dennis beat them down while Eyal Yanilov was escorted off the mats.

After it was over and while relieved chuckling was heard around the room, Jon stated that at the end of the day 10 people would be chosen personally by Eyal to fight the Predators in front of everyone....if they wanted to. To be picked you had to have somehow caught Eyal's eye and shown determination, or skill, or dedication, or all three.

Immediately my mind went into hyperdrive. I was nervous anyway and this news just helped to kick the hornets' nest right over. The little gremlin in my head was nattering at full speed.

"What if I got picked? I'm not a good sparrer or fighter, that I know. I've had counseling around my reluctance to fight. What if I'm picked? WHAT IF I'M PICKED?!! Huge honour though it would be maybe it would be better if I offered it to someone like Lewis Turpin from my club. After all, he's a blood descendent of former world champion boxer Randolph Turpin and can fight for England. Yes, much better if I offer the opportunity away. I mean, I don't want to embarrass my club do I?

Think of the humiliation of just freezing with your hands down in front of the worldwide head of KMG, the head of KMG UK, my own club's chief instructor, one of my own club's other instructors, plus about 10 guys from my club? I'm not a fighter and that's all there is to it. To have to go up in front of everyone like that would overwhelm me. It'd be like being in the Coliseum in ancient Rome. Yes, much better to give that offer away should it come my way. After all, Lewis or Al or Tomasz would put on a much better show than I ever could."

Looking back on it, my nervousness at the whole event

was simply finding outlets in order to purge some of the negative energy. What I've found through my life is that my mind will uncover ways to deal with stress and anxiety but divert from the actual issue that is causing it. So, before my P4 grading in March 2014 I was nervous about everything from work to my cat to the price of petrol in Tesco. As a child I was told that I should suppress all negative emotion and that a "sulky face" brought the mood down for those around me and would not get me any friends. Better to have a "smile on my little face" and smother all that negative feeling so other people wouldn't feel put off by me.

The mind in its complexity can't handle the above scenario and what happened was my brain simply found other things to vent the stress on to.

Step back and look at this for a moment.

I'm at a Krav Maga seminar with guys from my club. Several high ranking "officers" of the organisation I belong to are in the same room as me. There's a lot of people training that day.

Eyal Yanilov was a myth up to that point. Someone I'd only seen on the P1 to P4 DVDs or on photos on the Facebook group. Now I was in his presence. It was overwhelming. As adolescent as this sounds, it was how I felt and right or wrong we can't control HOW we feel. We can however control how we react to those feelings.

As the day wore on we worked up a sweat and when it got to about half an hour before finishing time we sat on the floor chatting and I could see Eyal walking around and tapping people on the shoulder. I was next to my club's instructor Al, who I'd been training with. Butterflies began to fly in erratic patterns in my stomach. The "selection" was happening. The people selected would move to the mats in the middle of the room. I tried to ignore what was going on. I didn't want to "stand out" in any way and run the gauntlet of being picked while Eyal was roaming around choosing people. The little voice in my head went off again.

"You can still offer this to Lewis. Anyway he's more likely to pick Al than you. Just look at the floor and try not to breathe or move until he's gone past. They've chosen 8 or 9 by now anyway so you won't get picked. Just keep staring at the floor and you'll be fine, just don't look up, whatever you do don't look......"

Out of the corner of my eye I could see Eyal's legs next to me. I heard him say "We need one more". I looked up and he was looking right at me. Smiling he asked "Do you want to do it?"

I replied "Oh yes!!" and practically leapt to my feet. As I walked to join the others I heard Al say, "Go for it Lance!"

We were taken to one side by Wayne Hubball and the rules of what was about to happen were explained. Each of us would go up one at a time against BOTH Predators with Alan Dennis as the referee/ invigilator to make certain things didn't get out of hand.

The point of this was to see how we reacted under adrenalin based scenarios with little or no time to think. While he was talking I could feel my anxiety branching off and sprouting leaves in areas I hadn't known existed 10 minutes previously. Everyone else gathered around the mats and I tried to keep my eyes focused on no one in particular. I was now beyond nervous.

As we lined up I stood at what I thought was going to be the first position but the other end of the line got to go first, meaning I would be the last one to fight.

Shit!

At my club I always try to go first or second on pressure drills or scenarios where fear can be debilitating, to simply get it out of the way and not let my imagination run riot.

Shit!

As the fights began it looked scary. The bullet men didn't go easy on anybody. One guy was beasted by them and some actually "lost" the fights they got into. As the minutes dragged on and felt like hours, only pride was keeping me from walking out. I was scared beyond measure.

Finally it was my go and Alan introduced me to

everyone and I got a round of applause. I couldn't look at anyone from my club because I thought that would make me feel even worse. Alan briefed the Predators on what to do and then whispered to me that they were going to try and box me in and I had to initially verbally communicate to try and stop it. My heart was pounding and I was trying to keep a stone face.

As the Predators approached me I tried to talk them down and my voice seemed to croak out of my throat. The fight kicked off and I was jumped by the second Predator from behind.

Everyone was cheering and as we tussled I managed to get on top of him and straddled him with my legs wide so he couldn't tip me off. I could hear cries of "Kick him in the bollocks!" and "In the head! In the head!"

Finally it was over and Alan pulled me off the guy. It felt like about 10 minutes had passed but in reality the fight lasted about a minute. Now it was over I felt good. The nerves were gone and the annoying gremlin voice was nowhere to be heard. All those nerves and stress and above all FEAR had tested my courage more than the fight itself.

Afterwards someone said I looked "Well ready for it" and a good mate from my club said that my nervousness hadn't showed and " The trademark Manley swagger said 'I'm ready for this shit, bring it on'. Time to give your hypnotherapist a bonus." I hadn't felt like that at all, I had in fact been scared out of my wits.

What this made me realise is that some of the most stone faced fighters in my club are probably just as scared as I was when in similar situations.

Fear can indeed show you where the edge is. It just needs taming first.

## The Gold Arrow

10th March 2015

I was going to write this in about 2 weeks. Probably a couple of days after my P5 grading on 21st March at Hengrove Park leisure centre in Bristol.

However....

Writing it now reflects how I feel now and not how I might feel after the grading. My feelings are specific now. If I pass, my feelings will be euphoric. If I fail they will be downbeat. Beyond that I don't know. This blog is about now.

When I took P4 I was almost sick with anxiety. I desperately wanted it and regarded the stamp in my passport as a licence to stay in the Big Boys' club. P1 and P2 are, in my opinion, foundation grades. P3 and up are where the screws tighten. P4 was more than just a different patch. To me it was approval, acceptance and certification of not only my skills at that level but that I could reach as high as people I had always considered to be beyond attainment. It was a tick in a box that said "Good Enough."

I took the grading stressed beyond measure and my worries weren't grounded in fear of physical injury or my energy giving out. They were formed in a void of desperately wanting validation. I remember sitting on the floor waiting for my results and thinking that if I failed I would never grade again. I felt that if I couldn't make the Silver Arrow of P4 then what was the point of trying any more? My attempt had been invalidated.

Like a lot of people I need to feel approved of.

I want that acceptance that comes from certifying life's tasks. As a Cub Scout in the 1980s I buzzed with a fierce pride at attaining the Gold Arrow while holding the rank of Sixer. I felt that these badges proved to me, my parents, my Akela and anyone who saw my green jersey, that I was someone who had tried and succeeded. The message of the Cub Scouts organisation had somehow got lost in my desire to get to the highest grade possible. While I helped old people, did 'Bob a Job' yearly and tried to be helpful it wasn't for love of aiding my fellow humans. It was to add points to a tally that would one day gain me that elusive and wonderful four bar patch (Sixer) on my arm and the Gold Arrow on my chest.

When I took P4 it was different to the previous three gradings. I went to London Copperbox arena to gain that patch to prove to myself and the world that I could rise higher. I never even realised this at the time but my motivation for that trip was solely to be able to say "Done that!"

In 2013 I took the PADI Rescue Diver course in Plakias,

Crete. The actual test was crazy with me in control of six separate people including another diver, and having to personally bring up and deal with an "unconscious" diver. The skills required were hard to master, the stress levels were high and my adrenal gland was waving a white flag. The examiner/ diving club owner had specifically told me that if I bollocksed it up she would not hesitate to fail me. I passed and felt elated. But then I lost interest in diving. I didn't really think too much about it at the time but it was because I had my Gold Arrow. With only 17 dives under my belt I had achieved a high rank. It would look nice on my CV. Job done. Mission accomplished.

This week I've realised that I had booked P5 with the same mentality and, had I not sat down and thought about it, once I passed I would have probably let my Krav training drift and become sporadic. My fitness levels sliding slowly into a different size of jeans. After all, five bars on a patch looks much nicer than the one I'll get on the next level!!!

Now, the only validation I want is that of my chief instructor at Krav Maga Midlands and my own. If I pass the P5 test in ten days and I will of course be happy. Fail and I'll be sad and also jealous of those who make it, but I will, for the first time be able to look at it as a learning experience and not another Gold Arrow that looked so very pretty. If I'm not successful I will come back in

October and try again.

The freedom and ease this realisation has brought me can't be described. I no longer want to be at that grading for any reason other than personal pride and to learn.

## The Seether

18th March 2015

As my P5 exam looms ever closer, I find myself lapsing into the type of behaviour that I indulged in just before P4, a year ago.

Bitten nails, wandering around the flat aimlessly, even more time spent on Facebook than normal, watching movies, tidying up without a real reason to and above all...worrying.

Today I was listening to some older music from my collection that I haven't played in a while. Awesome band Veruca Salt released a song back in the 90s called "The Seether." In it the singer Louise describes the rage monster that she becomes when angry. She admitted in interviews that this was something she found unable to control and would say the most terrible things to her family and friends. The song talks about "keeping her on a short leash" and "trying to knock her out" but nothing can stop 'The Seether'.

Louise said she regarded it as something that overcame her and made her something totally, utterly alien to her normal self. She hated how she became, but like a female Hulk sometimes her moods just could not be controlled.

My Seether is a bit less aggressive, but still a

distraction. It takes over my life and makes me fret about meaningless shit. My P5 grading is important to me but failing it is NOT the end of the world. I'll repeat that for myself:

FAILING IT IS NOT THE END OF THE WORLD.

Even typing those words I can feel my Seether getting a bit confused.

After all, he/ it sat with me loyally in the run up to P4 and dutifully got me to bite my nails to red ruin; end up taking double my prescribed dosage of beta blockers; and get Oxford Dictionary Ltd to phone me up asking if I'd like to be the poster boy for the definition of the word "stress".

Today I also read an excellent and reassuring article by Jon Bullock, head of KMG UK. He gives a lot of good advice about how to approach a grading with the right mindset.

My Seether is a blunt instrument and not the most intelligent of beasts. It takes all that worry and nerves and outsources them to other areas of my life. In the days before a grading I will find myself wondering if I've got enough cat litter in the house. I'll procrastinate over the fact that I have only two tins of baked beans instead of three. I'll even worry about whether or not to replace my toothbrush.

My Seether isn't as extreme as Louise's but it's still

there. Tonight I was mirroring the P5 techniques via the DVD on my telly, and got to the bit where Eyal Yanilov is talking about breathing techniques to remain calm and focused. He pointedly says that if you can control your emotions you will learn to "control the fight."

My Seether makes me a shadow of the man I want to be. It makes me dithery, unfocused, tired and panicky. It takes a wonderful experience like a Krav Maga grading and turns it into a court room appearance for a murder charge.

I will now reabsorb my Seether and change it into something called The Foundation. It will aid me in the run up to my grading in three days with a few nerves but more a supportive way of eating healthily, sleeping adequately and keeping myself fit for the day.

The Seether isn't a bastard. It does what it's programmed to do. It can however be retrained so it's not debilitating but an asset.

## Foregone

25th March 2015

On Saturday 21st March 2015 I took my P5 examination but I didn't pass it.

After a grueling test, as me and the other nine P5 candidates sat on the floor around examiner Nadav Shosan while the sweat dried on our sodden T-shirts and we sipped water from partially crushed plastic bottles, the atmosphere was tense. He briefly broke down exactly what we'd done wrong as a group and then moved on to individual feedback and scores.

I was last up (there is a yin and a yang to being the last one in the line up. During the exam, you get to see what everyone else is doing but you also have to wait a while to know your result). He looked at me and said flatly. "You need to retest everything. The spirit is there, the heart is there...but not the technique."

As previous postings on this blog have shown, I had spent time preparing both physically and mentally for the grading and was determined to take the news, either good or bad, with dignity and a positive attitude.

Nadav elaborated that I needed to work on self defence and weapons again. I replied "Do I want to know my score?" and after totting up the individual marks he said

"You got 66%".

The minimum pass is 70%. I smiled and said "I'll be back in October" which got a pat on the back from my grading partner and a round of applause from the other P5 candidates. I felt I had prepared well. I'd spent as much time as I could in front of the TV watching the P5 DVD and practicing the moves.

I'd been to the revision sessions at my club and had abstained from alcohol for a week before the testing.

I'd gone to bed early with a healthy, carb-heavy meal the night before and had done yoga and a cardio based regime at the gym for five weeks prior.

The test itself was a mixture of P4 and P5 stuff. My problem was that I'd not revised any of my P4 material and hadn't really touched it since October of last year. I knew I was making mistakes when tested on the moves but hoped the other areas would pull me through.

The sparring was the usual gruel fest. Seven rounds of 2 minutes, slightly different scenarios each time. By round 5 I had spat my gum shield out at least twice as I was struggling to breathe. After that we had ten rounds of 4 vs. 1, with two turns as the defender and 8 as an attacker holding a stick, a knife or a strike shield.

Unlike my P4 exam where I had sat waiting for my results with certain petulance about not coming back if I failed, I was pleased that this time my genuine mindset was one of acceptance and a desire to return at a later date and pass. I didn't feel bitter, or sad or angry. I was disappointed and felt the pangs as I watched the other guys get their certificates and patches.

But overall...thanks to a mixture of hard work; reading articles on both how to approach gradings and how to deal with fear; determination to give it my all and acceptance of whichever result I was to receive.

This time the work I did, unlike on the previous four gradings, didn't get me the new patch. What it did do however was help me to evolve. To accept feedback from the examiner at face value. To believe that my score was fair.

To know that I could come back in six short months and try again.

Above all....to take the experience as one of learning and improvement of my skills.

Nadav told me privately afterwards that my P5 stuff was OK but the P4 stuff had let me down. He also gave me a massive ego boost when he said I'd got 8 out of 10 for my fighting...even though this is the one area I thought I was weakest on. Fact he had mentioned twice how much I had my hands down during the bouts meant that the high score was for how I approached the fights, not my skills as a fighter.

This was overall a disappointment but I regard it as

something that has helped me to accept and to learn, and for that the experience was invaluable.

## Practitioner 2 to 5 Gradings
## Hengrove Park Leisure Centre, Bristol

26th March 2015

*(Blog about the gradings, that appeared on KMM's website. Some of the material in this is the same as "Foregone").*

Gearing up for a Practitioner level exam is always both fun and a bit stressful. At Krav Maga Midlands we spent the last four weeks getting ready with entire lessons focusing on grading revision.

With the Practitioner 1 exams now being held in-house, there were less people making the trip to Bristol (21st) or London (22nd) this time. We had four for each for P2, P3, and P4 with myself and another guy striving for P5.

I had arranged to share a ride down with Viesturs who was taking P4 and as we weren't on the mats until 2pm we had arranged to set off at 10.30. However at about 9 o'clock I checked Facebook to see messages from the P2 and P3 guys warning that there had been a bad accident on the M5 motorway closing off several junctions.

With 15 minutes to spare we got to Harlow Leisurezone to see the P2s and P3s gulping down some water and chatting, red faced, to our instructors Al, Bartosz and Russell, while they waited to be called for their results. Goz Gozwell from the Solihull and Kings Heath branches of KMM was waiting along and said it had gone well and she was now just hoping for a good result.

As the 2s and 3s then moved into huddles on the floor to receive their feedback and scores, me and the other 4s and 5s began to get kitted up. A short while later our club members came back, all holding certificates and patches and smiling.

It was reassuring to see that all our mates had got through.

Goz particularly was super happy, as was her instructor Al Natrins. As they made their way out we began to move into the vacant space to get ready. Alan Dennis took us for a quick warm up where he would intermittently shout "You ready?" to which we had to shout back "ALWAYS!!!" After cooking up a good sweat we then moved into positions for the actual grading.

There were ten of us for P5. Me and the other bloke from KMM had agreed to pair with people we didn't know rather than each other, to keep us sharp and focused. I got to partner a lad from Nick Maison's Total Krav Maga. We began to go through the moves with Nadav Shoshan from the KMG HQ team in Israel as our examiner.

Me and my partner were last in the line up so we

noticed pretty quickly that people further up the queue were being handed sticks and knives. This was P4 revision that they had put amongst the P5 curriculum. We moved through hair grabs and bear hugs before then doing stick defences and stabbing attacks. I hadn't revised the P4 material and was worried that this would let me down. Once we'd worked through ground releases Nadav then told us to get our 16oz gloves on for the sparring. My P4 test had sparring that was grueling to say the least. As we got into a huddle to hear our instructions, Nadav said that we would fight seven rounds of 2 minutes each, changing partners each time. He added that we were to go as hard as our partners "allowed us to" but not any harder.

Message being: It's a fight but don't try to kill each other.

The first round was designated as two for two, meaning a jab + a cross from one before the opponent could respond in kind. This round wasn't too bad but then we moved to harder rounds such as up close and personal (grappling range) and then the expected "free for alls."

The exhaustion factor of this type of fighting cannot be easily portrayed in words. I had been hitting the gym for some serious cardio workouts the last 4 or 5 weeks and even then my energy levels just about coped. Unlike in movies, when you fight constantly for 2 minute rounds with only a thirty second break, your vigour quickly dissipates and only willpower can keep you upright and striking. Nadav made it quite clear that this was a test of resilience and time to "suck it up and carry on." I had to spit out my gum shield on two occasions as I couldn't breathe properly and the order to "try and take your partner to the floor" invariably led to a lot of grunting and struggling as exhausted fighters tried to heave each other over and down. Once that was finally out the way we moved to 4 against 1. This worked out nicely as there was ten of us, in two groups.

One guy was in the middle with someone holding a knife, another a stick, a third a strike shield and the final guy trying to strangle. My club mate was up first and put up a good fight. This lasted 75 seconds with no break before number 2 was in place, which was me. I had imagined this wouldn't be quite so bad as the previous fighting but coupled with how tired we already were the whole thing was knackering. We had to go twice in the middle, as well as being an attacker on the other rounds. Finally the whole thing was over and we dragged ourselves upstairs to get our results and swap our sodden T-shirt for fresh ones.

As we sat on the floor and the sweat dried, Nadav demonstrated general areas where people had made mistakes such as bridging during ground releases and then moved to the scores. The first few people passed and you could see the relief on their faces as we gave them a round of applause.

About three guys got the "conditional pass" meaning their own instructors would hold onto their certificates and patches until they had performed one thing again to get the whole grade. I was last up and Nadav said "You need to retest everything. The spirit is there, the heart is there but not the technique."

I had mentally prepared for failure as much as for success in the run up to the grading and had promised myself that I would take either result with dignity and a positive mindset. Nadav added that my weapons and self defence work needed improvement. As the only P5 candidate to have not passed I was determined to remain cheerful and jokingly asked "Do I want to know my score?"

He replied "You got 66%".

As the pass mark is 70% I was still reassured that I had missed by only a small margin.

We then lined up for the awarding of the certificates and some photos. I approached Nadav afterwards to see what I'd failed on. He said "I don't consider this a fail" and pointed out that my P5 stuff was OK but the P4 stuff was lacking and at this level I can't have bad techniques in my repertoire. My ground work had been fine and the biggest boost was finding that he'd given me 8 out of 10 for my fighting, despite telling me that I had my hands down too much, a problem that had cost me a piece of a tooth at the P4 grading in 2014. As sparring is something I consider myself weak on it was greatly reassuring to find out I'd got such a high score.

I shook his hand and said I'd see him in October for the retest.

The first time I've failed a grading but the learning experience was invaluable and to have received such constructive criticism meant a great deal to me. Time to hit the floor in preparation for the October resit.

Bring it on.

## Krav Maga Sciocco

1st April 2015

*(April Fools' day prank that I played on Facebook and a LOT of people fell for)*

Hi guys,

Happy to announce that today I moved from KMG to KMS (Krav Maga Sciocco) who are a new club in Coventry, UK. I took their P5 test today and got a score of 99% (lost 1% as apparently my hair grab was a bit over zealous. My partner now has a bald patch). Cost £354 to do their P5 exam but it only lasted 35 minutes and the chief instructor ("Sir" as we call him) has assured me that with the right level of investment I will be an Expert 5 by December next year, provided I can raise the £2500 that the test costs.

Thanks to all the guys who've shared my journey so far with me with KMG, and if you fancy a faster option to get to the higher grades then why not check out Krav Maga Sciocco.

Kida!

## Anna & Cassandra- A Story

8th April 2015

"I had a really good time mummy, we all learned how to sing "The Wheels on the Bus".

Cassandra was nattering as normal, the way she always did after playschool. Anna was happy that her daughter was in such a chirpy mood. Last few sessions she'd been a bit grizzly when she picked her up. The teachers had put forward the idea that she was having a good time and Anna had to concur. She'd hated going home when she was a little girl but it was for different reasons.

Cassandra held up the piece of paper covered in paint. "I made this too mummy" she said proudly, then paused looking up expectantly.

"Very nice my darling, is it a car?"

Cassandra looked cross and tutted. "No silly, it's you mummy!"

Anna laughed and ruffled her daughter's hair. "I know sweetie, I'm just playing."

Cassandra giggled as they reached the car. Anna held her daughter's hand tightly as they crossed the road to where she'd left the vehicle. Anna didn't like parking in the cul-de-sac but the road near the school had been full as always. She handed the keys down. "OK Madame, do your magic."

Cassandra giggled again and with some concentration used her tiny fingers to activate the door locks. She smiled approvingly as the indicator lights flashed and the car beeped.

"Good girl, now let's get you strapped in."

Anna opened the door and pulled the harness open on the child seat in the back, removing a half squashed Ribena carton from the cushion. She lifted Cassandra up gently and put her down, strapping her in and checking the belt was secure.

As she closed the door and went to step to the driver's side she felt a hand on her shoulder and a rasping voice went "Don't move, I'll cut you!"

Anna's breath caught in her throat. Her body tensed and she glanced down as a sharp pressure was in her right side, just below her ribs. The man behind her pushed her up against the side of the car, holding the back of her head with one hand. He hissed to someone else, "Quick, go on."

Anna twisted her head to look as a scruffy man with too much stubble and an old torn jacket yanked the door open where Cassandra was sitting.

"Mummy, what's going on?" her daughter shouted out, her eyes going wide.

"It's OK baby, just be quiet please."

The hand on her head was holding her tightly, she struggled to control her breathing. She could still feel the pressure in her side. The other man grabbed her handbag and leaned in over Cassandra, checking the foot wells and the seats. Cassandra started to cry. "Mummy!" She looked terrified. Anna could smell both of them. They reeked of body odour and too much booze. And something else...something rotten. Trying to control her breathing and remain calm she said in as controlled a voice as she could manage.

"Take what you want, just don't hurt my daughter please."

The man behind her hissed back "I said shut up and be quiet you whore."

"That's it" the second man said.

"Check the front. Quick before someone comes."

The man moved round the passenger side of the car, checking around him in case anyone could see them. Cassandra was crying louder. As the man yanked open the opposite side door and began to rummage through the glovebox the voice behind her said "That watch you're wearing, take it off and give it me."

Anna trembled with fear but managed to stay steady on her feet. The pressure on her head released slightly and she reached over to unfasten the strap on her watch. She handed it back over her shoulder. "Nice" the voice whispered, then said to the other man "Come on!"

"Done, nothing else."

"You've been really good, thanks. You might want to teach your little bitch to be quiet. Hopefully we'll see you again."

As he spoke his other hand moved down and squeezed Anna's breast and he laughed. Time froze. The roughness of his fingers. The sound of Cassandra crying. The other man moving back around to join his friend. The street light fifty yards away casting a spattery reflection on the car's wet black roof. But above all Anna remembered her father, wanting to "play" with his daughter when he came home drunk and Anna's mother could do nothing to stop him.

With a snarl she whirled against the pressure in her right side, her forearm smashing into the man's wrist. He yelped in pain and his knife went skittering across the tarmac. Before he could react Anna grabbed his head with both hands and pulled down hard, bringing her knee up into his face, once, twice, three times. His nose shattered and blood sprayed.

With a gurgle he fell forward and then rolled onto his back. Anna stamped down on his crotch with her heel twice, hard.

In the five seconds this had taken the other man had iced up. He stared at them both. Cassandra was still wailing loudly. "What the....?!!" he mouthed, clutching Anna's bag. She turned to face him and he gulped.

"Now look lady, I don't want any trouble." Anna advanced on him, stepping over the twitching, bloodied man at her feet. "Stay back, look I'm sorry." He dropped the handbag in the road and tried to turn but Anna grabbed his shoulders and span him around, slamming him into the car. He screeched as Anna kicked him hard in the knee, his leg buckling. She rained her fists down on his head, once, twice, three times until he collapsed in the road.

Breathing heavily she looked around. Left, right, behind her. Standing twenty yards away was another woman, older, her mouth open. After a long moment she stammered, "I...saw...I...do you need any help my dear?"

Anna gasped and cleared her throat.

"Call the police and an ambulance. Do it now." The woman nodded and reached for her mobile, staring in horror at Anna and the two men.

She opened the back door and leaned in. Cassandra was screaming her head off.

"Shhh, baby it's alright." She unclipped the safety harness and pulled her daughter clear, stepping away from the unconscious man laying at her feet.

Cassandra stopped screaming but was still sobbing as Anna hugged her into her shoulder. "It's alright baby, shhhh, it's alright."

After a couple of minutes Cassandra's sobs began to quieten.

In the distance they could hear sirens.

## Six

### 13th April 2015

About 3 weeks ago I took P5 and failed it.

I'm not mentioning that for an attempt at sympathy. I took the news with a dignity that I'm proud of and promised to return in October to do it all again.

Problem is...October seems soooo far away right now.

I mean, I have a holiday for a whole MONTH in Crete between now and then. To be precise, from June to July. And THAT seems far away too. October will be when the warm weather we are only just now starting to enjoy, is going to be on its way out and Autumn in all its nauseating shades of orange is cosying up to introduce its bigger brother Winter.

From P1 to P5 I have noticed just how fast time flew between the gradings. Main reason being that I have a thing called a "life" that gets between a twice yearly visit to London or Bristol.

In the run up to my P5 test, I had the following "regime".

1. Yoga at least twice a week.

2. Krav at least twice a week.

3. Cardio based workout (tailored for me by a personal trainer at my gym) two or three times a week.

4. Watching the P5 DVD on my TV at home and copying the moves (except the break falls or rolls).

I did this for about 5 weeks. Determined to go in as prepared as possible. The examiner told me after that what let me down was my P4 stuff (which I hadn't revised). So, back to the revision with some P4 stuff (and in case they pull a flanking maneuver at the next grading, P2 and P3 as well).

Thing is....

I have been attending the gym for the cardio stuff BUT I'm going a maximum of twice a week to do that. I go to Krav once a week and I haven't looked at the P5 DVD since I got back.

While I have hardly become slothful, that exuberance and lust for the 5th bar on the patch has now had the volume turned down somewhat.

It is very hard to maintain that kind of momentum, especially half a year away from a retake. I don't even think it's necessary to keep the same fitness levels sustained BUT I also know that I need to keep on top of things.

Jon Bullock and a lot of examiners and instructors I've met over the 3 years I've been with KMG had said that the worst thing you can do is rest on your laurels and become lazy after passing a grading. Like any skill set, Krav techniques need to be practiced to be kept fresh.

October is now 3 weeks nearer than it was when I took that grading.

I shall maintain a healthy balance between now and then.

Nuff said.

## How The Flinch Stole Combat

### 14th April 2015

I love Krav Maga. I've been a member of Krav Maga Midlands since March 2012 and I find the sport to be exactly what I need to both keep fit and to increase my confidence.

The technical side of Krav, I think is brilliant. Love the knife and gun techniques, the different kicks, the tactics and the innovation. I also get a buzz out of the pressure drills and scenarios such as the Tunnel of Fun (8+ guys standing either side of a narrow corridor, you try and walk to the other end) or Zombies or Multiple Attackers or Slow Fighting. The list goes on.

However, something that I always had an issue with is the combat side of Krav Maga.

At a grading I have no problem with fighting and will get stuck in. A pleasant memory is during the sparring at the end of my P3 test, an unknown instructor was stood by the side of the mats cheering me on with "Yes, hit him. Don't forget your feet! Good, keep going!"

Turned out to be Jon Bullock, head of KMG UK.

But…something that always proved to be a "Marmite" moment was coldly padding up and sparring with someone at a class designed solely for combat. It was like a switch was thrown in my head from Like to Dislike.

There are many tried and tested methods to deal with this type of thing. I tried most of them.

I'd make myself go. I'd be determined to enjoy myself. I'd partner the biggest guy in the room. I'd partner a higher grade. I'd meditate. I'd talk to other students or instructors. I'd try and rationalise and analyse why this was happening. I'd "man up" and "grow a pair".

Nothing worked long term.

At most I'd get a couple of sessions before the Dislike switch was thrown again. This situation was irritating to say the least. I really WANTED to like it, but something within me wasn't having any of it. Like anchovies on pizza or Marmite on toast…it was a black and white situation with absolutely no grey. Love it or hate it. I hated it.

Bottom line was that I was getting frustrated and feeling like a pansy. The sensation was the same as the first time I went cliff jumping. Standing at the edge, looking down at the water…and for 15 minutes unable to jump off. Even though I knew there was virtually no danger in it, every instinct was screaming at me to back away. I finally did it and never looked back. But with sparring…things didn't improve no matter what I tried in order to overcome the issue. My reluctance was like one gigantic flinch.

I eventually realised that the issues were probably

emotional and/ or psychological. When we fought I'd perceive my partner and the other fighters in the room as malicious and out to hurt me, even though I knew they weren't. Before my P4 grading I was genuinely uncertain as to whether or not I'd pass it.

I was effectively "winging it" and I realised that I'd never make G level if I couldn't get my head fixed. It was then that I decided that I had to overcome this. A friend of mine recommended hypnotherapy as her son had taken a few sessions years ago, to deal with unresolved issues from his childhood. I contacted a woman named Rebecca Bedford who gave me a free initial meeting to lay the groundwork for what I wanted resolved. When I came back I was genuinely surprised that you are not actually "hypnotised" like in movies. Instead the process could best be described as "guided meditation".

I closed my eyes while relaxing music was playing and Rebecca talked me through some mental imagery and told me to imagine that I was in a safe location such as a beach that was my private place of solitude. She then got me to remember certain events and said to "link it on" to whatever thought came up next, regardless of how silly, unusual, or out of place that thought might appear.

I had about five or six sessions in total where we slowly moved through the knots and creases in my psyche. It turned out that I had deep rooted fears of humiliation and rejection. I also had felt frustrated as a child through being forced to pretend everything was OK when it wasn't and believing I didn't have the right to express my opinions. Most crucially, I had made a decision as a very young boy that I would never be able to compete with "bigger boys" as they were stronger, faster and better than me. All of this had gone into the blender of my subconscious and affected my ability to relax and enjoy training.

After the final session I attended both a sparring session and contact combat in the same week. For the first time ever I actually enjoyed myself and thought it was fun. I held off writing this article for a week just in case there was some kind of emotional relapse and there wasn't. The answers to what was holding me back were locked away inside my head, and finally I had found the key. There was no epiphanous moment. No sudden revelation or jolt of clarity. It was simply that I looked on the same situations with a different set of feelings than I had before.

## Fragility

25th April 2015

Last night I momentarily thought I'd dislocated/ broken/ sprained another finger during Krav training.

Last October I got booted in the left hand and my pinky went a bit banana shaped. I was out of training for more than 2 months and missed both P camp and my P5 grading as a result.

All for the least useful appendage on my body.

Yesterday we were doing knife threats and as I whirled to knock the hand of my partner away with my right arm, I somehow managed to jab my ring finger right into the bone on her forearm. Unlike the last time, this bloody hurt and in between cursing I frantically ripped off my MMA mitt in case I had another busted joint.

Could still flex and grip but it hurt like a bastard, so I stepped out for a minute to see how I felt and let the pain ebb. This was at 8.20pm, with the class wrapping up at half eight. We were about to move to a final pressure drill, something I nearly always enjoy.

I had a choice to make.

Either....

1). Go back in, "sucking up" my discomfort and pain and give it my all.

2). Take a back seat and miss the final drill, in case I tempt fate too far and end up really hurting myself.

Something I've realised in the 3+ years I've been doing Krav is that it is very easy to get hurt, either by mistake, misfortune or bad technique application. The human body is a delicate machine and toes & fingers are fragile little things.

I've done gradings up to P5 with some severe fighting and an exhaustion factor that is hard to imagine...but ultimately we are padded up with shin guards, gum shields and 16oz gloves. There is a sense of caution present at all times.

Krav teaches us to be more than just people who fight. It talks about walking or running away if we can when faced with potential violence and above all putting your safety first. While I always imagined injuries sustained in training would be for reasons of macho sparring or taking on a bigger opponent, a wonky finger caused by a 16 year old girl's forearm wasn't on my list of heroic wounds. However, as I stood there with an ice pack clenched around my throbbing digit watching the others throwing punches for a tabata workout...I realised as my breathing returned to normal that I'd made the right decision.

My body needs respect too and listening to it when it starts complaining is a discipline that I need to keep practicing. I've seen a G5 instructor get a cracked rib during a grading and simply carry on. While I have a lot of respect for him for that, part of me still wonders what would have happened if he'd got thumped in the same rib twice.

We've all seen boxing matches where one or both fighters are busted up, eyes like slits, faces purple and puffy but they keep going out of dogged determination.

I don't do Krav to prove I'm tough. I do it to keep fit and to give me an "edge" if I'm ever attacked on the street for real. I like the skills Krav gives me but as I've grown older I feel less and less like I need to prove I'm "hard" by going beyond my own pain threshold and then carrying on. And by that I mean pain from injury, not pain through exhaustion or fatigue.

Adrenaline is one thing but there's a time where I would rather feel embarrassed and disappointed but not carry on, than do something that might put me out of training for a lot longer.

## Patience

### 6th May 2015

I found out in 2002 that my left knee was bereft of its anterior crusciate ligament. I was doing kickboxing and fighting with the instructor of the club. I tried to pivot on the left leg and instead of using the ball of my foot I kept it flat, meaning a noise like a lettuce being hacked with a knife reverberated through my body. I limped off to the side and had a knee the size of a grapefruit for about a week.

In 2004 I went for an operation at a hospital in London and the consultant surgeon (a bloke I'd only seen at a distance up to that point) turned up in his gold watch and Saville Row suit and manipulated my leg. After asking "Does this hurt?" a few times, he then pronounced that my leg was perfectly healthy, I didn't need surgery and to go home.

Happily I skipped home, smiling like a spoiled child on Xmas morning, as I naively believed the ACL had somehow grown back of its own accord.

It turned out that because I was doing a load of cycling in London, the knee had compensated for the missing ligament by growing lots of muscle and the leg was stable enough to not warrant the operation. Basically, that doctor was saving the NHS a few quid.

Years later and the issue turned up to haunt me. I was rejected without interview for both the Postal & Courier Regiment of the Logistics Corp of the British Army and the RAF Reservists for this. As soon as my medical history was seen, they didn't want to know.

The TA major in charge of recruitment spoke to me at length on the phone and said "Once you're in, you can get as injured as you want... but if they let you in with an existing injury you might sue them...and they don't want that."

I can't go jogging because the next day the knee is sore and swollen. A physio I go to occasionally said not to run but cycle instead and compared my knee to tectonic plates below San Franciso. They grind together and occasionally that causes issues on the surface.

In Krav Maga the knee has proved to be a nuisance. If I grade then it's swollen like a bastard but I have learned to adapt by taking painkillers before and after (including anti inflammatory pills like Diclofenac) and also wearing not one but TWO knee braces (a medical one and a Poundland blue/ black thingy). This has meant the knee is manageable in the short term BUT my flexibility is fucking awful in my lower body and kicks from my left leg can be like Bambi trying to stand up, especially if I'm tired. I can't kneel on my heels as it is beyond painful.

It's basically kind of sucky.

Recently I went to a doctor who referred me to hospital, who sent me for an MRI scan who then called me in to see a nurse in the Fracture Clinic. She said the knee can be repaired, the operation waiting time is a maximum of 15 weeks and I will be discharged the same day. The knee will then be healthy and I can go jogging, do yoga like a boss and have the flexibility I've missed for 13 years.

However there's a downside.

When I get this done I will be out of training of ANY variety, be it Krav Maga, cardio or yoga...from between 6 to 12 months. The nurse specifically said the timeline would be:

Two weeks complete rest. Six weeks no driving. Six to twelve months no combat or training.

I failed P5 in March of this year and the next grading is in October. I've recently read about a discipline called Ghost Fighter, which maximises ability to hit, while minimising the chance of being hit back. That's right up my alley and I will attend my "taster" class next Monday to see if I like it. I've kept my cardio up to speed to deal with the abject misery that is the sparring of a P5 grading and have Wayne Hubball's Adrenaline coming up on June 6th.

Problem is that the hospital have offered me surgery and will only postpone for 6 months. That means I can go on my summer holiday from June to July for four weeks but I will have to then ask to go back on the waiting list...or lose my place completely. The operation will happen by September so if I have it I will miss my P5 resit.

There are a multitude of factors FOR doing this and a lot less for not. If I get my knee repaired I will (later) be stronger, fitter and have more endurance. My kicking from the left leg will be more powerful and I will be able to fight without worrying if my knee will go "click" at the wrong moment. I will have to wait until at least March 2016 for my P5 exam, remembering that I passed my P4 in March 2014.

Ultimately it's a question of priorities. I know that I need to be fully fit for a grading and for training and by being patient I can come back and aspire to G level and beyond. The brief satisfaction of getting my five bar patch with repairs pending, will not happen.

There's a time to be patient.

## The Grate Outdoors

12th May 2015

At KMM tonight we got shunted off to a much smaller room which can best be described as a shuttlecraft to a ship. The school we train at had double booked us and Chief Instructor Bartosz decided to make the most of the situation.

We'd used the smaller room before and the confined space is a mixed blessing. We lack the lovely spaciousness of the usual badminton court but the claustrophobic surroundings are great for some close quarter work and how to deal with limited range of movement.

The warm up consisted of the usual heavy stretching with some "moving between everyone else" stuff. We had to aim for heads and crotches with palm strikes while simultaneously trying to prevent anyone landing a slap on us. There were a couple of loud "clonks" as someone caught a wallop on the groin guard. Bartosz was heard to remark at one point "I love that sound!" which raised a laugh.

After a warm up we moved to hammer blows on focus mitts. One thing I've noticed with this kind of striking is that you need to keep your fists clenched tight. A few times I yelped as my wrist buckled and pain shot up my arm. Once we got that sorted we put the moves into combinations and then headed outside. The area at the back of that classroom is semi-enclosed, with a metal fence on one side and a brick wall and windows on the other. The tarmac road surface slopes up to an access area. Ideal for some improv. We got into pairs and went through close quarter strangle holds, i.e. when your attacker is right in your face with little or zero room to maneuver.

I got partnered with a much bigger lad who is a lot stronger than I am. A couple of times I was expecting him to use the wall to grate my face off. We drilled this and other movements, working in a "skipping kick" when being attacked from the side and then we had the final bit of fun.

Bartosz split us into two groups with guys dotted along the path leading up beside the classrooms and around the driveway. Some had plastic training knives, others strike shields and the rest their bare hands. We moved through one at a time and had to "simply get from one end to the other....twice." Getting shoved against a brick wall by a 17 stone, 6 feet 4 inch guy holding a strike shield can be tiring. I got my elbow cut on the second attempt and one of the attackers looked slightly narked when he grabbed my arm and drew his hand back to find his fingers had my blood on them. In the middle was a lad with a knife who'd scream for money, and up the top a couple who worked together with a strike shield and a knife, making it hard to get past them. I love this kind of pressure drill as there's no time to think and you have to react on instinct. After everyone had had at least two goes each, we finally wrapped things up.

Forming the line for the final kida, it was clear that someone had really got into the spirit of the thing, as one lad had a muddy footprint on his chest where he'd been booted away while trying to attack.

Great fun and educational and it's always enjoyable to do Krav outside when the nice weather kicks in.

## Chav Maga

14th May 2015

In the 4-ish years I've been doing Krav Maga, I've only had to use it twice in "real life". Once was while I was on holiday last summer in Crete. Very minor, no harm done and being drunk I fumbled what I intended to do but it worked anyway.

Today it happened again and like before, it wasn't a heroic battle between good and evil with me standing howling over the twitching corpse of my vanquished foe. It was solved through the lower scales of conflict resolution that we are taught in Krav training.

I was at work (I deliver stuff) and met a particularly unpleasant woman who refused to sign for a parcel for her neighbour and got lippy about various trivial stuff before marching back indoors with the words "I'm not arguing with you about it."

As I finished what I was doing I pulled the communal door to the apartments shut and it closed with a loud bang. Not my intention, but stuff happens.

As I got to the street there was an elderly couple standing near my van and the woman asked if I'd mind posting a letter for her.

"Well we don't normally but no problem my dear, I

don't mind doing...."

"DO YOU MIND NOT SLAMMING THE FRONT DOOR LIKE THAT?!! THE BABY'S ASLEEP!"

I turn to find the gobby woman standing fuming in the driveway leading to her apartment block. The old couple look embarrassed and I feel my temper fraying.

"I'm not talking to you, go away." I turn my back on her and resume my chat with the old couple.

"DON'T SLAM MY F***ING DOOR LIKE THAT, I'M REPORTING YOU TO YOUR COMPANY!!"

She slams the communal gate harder than I shut the front door, presumably determined to make certain her baby stays awake. I lose my rag, and yell after her:

"P**s off you f***ing silly cow!!!"

As I turn back to the old couple who are now silent with confusion and embarrassment, the gate creaks open again and I'm confronted with the sight of her boyfriend. He has a baseball cap on, baggy shorts, and a large, faded tattoo on his neck. He's also got his right hand stuck to the depth of his wrist...down the front of his shorts.

"What'd you say?" he mumbles.

I take my earphones from around my neck and put them in my pocket and sigh "You ARE joking me?!"

"What'd you say? The baby's sleeping, don't slam the f***ing door like that!!"

His atrocious missus then starts the predictable mantra.

"Leave it babe, babe...leave it...come inside babe!"

"You mind not holding your dick when you're talking to me?!"

He moves closer, still with his hand firmly gripping his knob and I take one step back with my right foot and put my arms up in the best 'Geoff Thompson' stance, left arm forward, right arm half extended, palms up.

"Back off, just stay away."

"Babe, come in. Leave it babe!"

"What you gonna do?!" he smirks, getting closer, when he makes contact with my left hand I shove him away.

"F**K OFF!!!"

He backs off but continues making threats as he moves away towards the gate. "What you gonna do?"

"Seriously mate, just get lost. What YOU gonna do anyway? Wipe the hand you've had your cock in on me?"

He glares at me from the gate with his hand still cuddling his genitals and then mumbles something more about what I think I'm going to do then disappears.

I turn back to the old couple, who are standing there silent and open mouthed.

"Sorry about that. More than happy to post your letter for you my love, you have a good day."

## Call of Duty: Ghost Fighter

22nd May 2015

Via Adrenaline's Wayne Hubball I found out about a different type of boxing discipline, Ghost Fighter. In a nutshell it is about avoiding getting hit, while being able to hit.

The blurb on the advertising states "Ghost Fighter Central (developed by Phil Norman)- Offers the latest in stealth fighting, a stand up fighting system which enables you to strike with minimal return from your opponent. This unorthodox system teaches you dynamic striking angles whilst utilising evasive movement, leaving the person in front of you hitting thin air and feeling like they are fighting a GHOST!"

Hmmm....

My cynicism was whispering in my ear. This sounded a lot like the Gun Kata from the Christian Bale movie "Equilibrium" (mathematically predicting where an opponent will fire at in a gun fight so you can move just before they shoot). I checked the Ghost Fighter website and their club T-shirts have the slogan "Now you see me...." on the front. In a list of reasons to try Ghost Fighter was the paragraph: "No more toe to toe. Gone are the days of using our heads as conkers taking hit after hit. The elusive movement of Ghost massively minimises hits".

Double hmmm....

But as I have some tiresome psychological stuff that prevents me from fully enjoying the sparring or fighting side of Krav Maga I thought I'd give it a look. I spoke to a guy named Ade on the phone. He's the only certified Ghost instructor in the Birmingham area and I was welcome to attend for a free lesson.

I made my way over to Acocks Green in Birmingham the following Monday and met him and his club members at a small gym. Ade is also a Krav Maga instructor of G2 level and splits his time between the two worlds. I chatted to a couple of guys who were warming up. They told me that the principles of Ghost have boosted their confidence in Krav, and the skills it teaches have given them an edge they didn't have before when fighting.

Talking to Ade he told me there are 4 rules in Ghost.

1). Don't enter No Man's Land.

2). Get off the track.

3). Continuous motion.

4). Don't get hit.

As we formed up in a line we did the Ghost version of Krav's "kida!" which was left foot forward, punch left fist into right palm and shout "respect!" Then we did some warming up to get a sweat on before splitting off into pairs. Ade got us to work on some striking, pointing out that in Ghost there is no sparring until you are advanced in the discipline, mainly as the whole point of Ghost is to avoid getting punched.

He then had one of each pair close their eyes and the partner stand within their reach. The "blind" one had to then throw punches while the other attempted to block. After we'd all had a go Ade explained that if you get too close to someone even a blind man will be able to land at least one punch on you. Therefore it's better to stay out of reach and not enter No Man's Land.

After some more workouts on striking we then moved to a specific technique designed to thwart someone attempting to use jabs. It took me and some of the others a while to crack this but I could see and feel the difference afterwards.

The idea is that as someone jabs you, you move your head back, you twist your upper body and "load" your left arm. You then switch stance by swapping your feet and duck around the jabbing fist, stepping to the left of your opponent. You are then in a blind spot and can deliver a hook punch to their face before stepping behind them to come full circle. I really liked this technique and with a lot of practice I could see that it would be useful.

I chatted to Ade afterwards and he broke down what the 4 principles are about.

"Don't enter No Man's Land. Which means don't enter

your head into anywhere where you can get hit. Get off the track means if you stay on the track with someone there's going to be a collision, someone's going to get hurt. Continuous motion means that a stationary target is a lot easier to hit than a moving target. And the fourth principle... if you forget about all of that just don't get hit."

From what I could see the basic benefits of Ghost Fighter to me would be that I would be able to approach my reluctance to sparring in a "David and Goliath" mentality as opposed to trying to emulate stronger, more experienced fighters. By that I mean that there are ways to solve problems that require lateral solutions and not direct confrontation. There are several guys in my Krav Maga club who are fast, strong and skilled when sparring. Meeting them head on is a mixed bag at the best of times. Working on my cardio from six weeks before my P5 grading helped me to sustain energy during the milling we had at the end (7 rounds of 2 minutes, full on. Then 10 rounds of 4 against 1. Two as the defender, eight as an attacker). By being fit enough to go the course I was able to keep slugging away and ended up with a score of 8 out of 10 for my sparring, despite failing the grading itself.

One thing I noticed during this grading was some guys simply locking up tight by keeping their faces protected but not hitting back in the later rounds. One bloke told me afterwards that he was "blowing out my arse" by about round 5 and felt unable to fight so just gritted his teeth and hung in till the end.

By having suitable cardio fitness levels plus an ability to be "sneaky" and work around other people's frontal strength I believe I would be able to stand my ground much better. The best example would be the tale of a double decker bus that came to a low bridge and was 6 inches too tall to go under it. Various methods were discussed as to how they could get the bus through. Turning it around or dismantling the bridge plus many other suggestions. After a while someone simply said "Why not let the tyres down and drive slowly under then inflate the tyres again?" I don't feel I will ever be able to face some fighters that I know head on and win. However, by adapting my fitness levels to have better endurance plus learning how to get on their flanks, I would feel a lot more confident about my future.

Overall the Ghost Fighter discipline is like an expansion pack on the Playstation or X-Box franchise "Call of Duty." You can buy extra levels featuring new battles with soldiers or even zombies. You can buy maps and equipment and cheat codes but none of them will mean anything unless you have a copy of the main game. Ghost will be useful to me as a bolt-on for my main Krav training.

I'll definitely be back.

## Adrenaline: The Breakout
## Krav Maga Global & FAST Defence UK
## Harlow Leisurezone, Essex, UK

*"Let Us Prey!"*

10th June 2015

Fast Defence UK has been around for about 30 years. Considered by many to be the "missing link" between self defence and martial arts training, FAST stands for "Fear, Adrenaline and Stress Training."

Their website states "FAST training empowers people by teaching how to manage the adrenaline release – no matter what the perceived threat and no matter what the context – and use it to create the most appropriate win." Most importantly it also says that training teaches people to "avoid, defuse and, if absolutely necessary, stop violence directed at them."

I had a taste of what this involves in June 2014 at the Krav Maga Global World Tour with Eyal Yanilov (KMG Chief Instructor). Me and 9 others got chosen by Master Eyal to fight what are known as the "predators". These are aggressive, violent and ferocious attackers who come out with verbal as well as physical assaults. The basis of the scenarios we entered can be boiled down to this:

"One or more guys are in your face. What are you going to do?"

Predator armour is unique in design in that it allows full freedom of movement for the person inside the "suit" but also allows their opponent/ victim to strike to the face, chest and groin as hard as they can. Adrenaline level 1 is based on one attacker and encourages the use of "tunnel vision" to retain focus on what is directly in front of you.

On Adrenaline 2, the game is changed in that you have multiple predators and have to deal with varying scenarios with between 2 and 5 attackers.

I'd been looking forward to this for several months and arrived early at Harlow Leisurezone. I met Andras Millward, Director of Instructor Development for FAST in the canteen. I asked him about FAST's recent surge in popularity and he said:

"There's been a big change, big upheaval in the FAST defence world. WE knew it worked but we weren't very good at telling the world it worked. A LOT of new people have come on board now. It's a lot stronger. Our relationship with Krav Maga Global is really helping our profile as well. We're like one of the best kept secrets in the world. Today we've got 50 to 55 students booked in. On Adrenaline 1 we had people coming here from abroad, countries like Switzerland, France and Norway. Our purpose today is to give you all more information about the adrenal release and response and then put you back in it again."

We kicked off just after 10.30am and Andras plus the head of Krav Maga Global UK, Jon Bullock spoke to us about what the day had in store. Then we had a lecture from Dr Kirsty Hunter, about the scientific aspects of the body's response to threat. We were told about the importance of correct breathing (inhale to belly, then chest through the nose, exhale through the mouth) and the different reactions to fear. She also told us about FAST's "A,B,C's" which stands for Awareness, Boundaries and Conflict Resolution (or Combatives).

Awareness means the ability to observe and accurately interpret stimuli within our environment and then identify and manage our own internal state.

Boundaries means knowing how and when to establish recognisable physical and/or emotional boundaries, and is considered essential to what FAST teaches. Combatives covers situations that require physical self-defence and provides simple and effective techniques that can be learnt and applied successfully by all, irrespective of age or sex.

After Dr Hunter had spoken to us we then moved into the preliminary phase of the training, the "woofing."

Woofing refers to where people are threatening or verbally aggressive in order to test boundaries. Like a dog barking, the expression describes how people can behave when trying to intimidate or even attack others. We were told that body language is VERY important for us in these scenarios. You are taught to stand with your feet steady but NOT to assume a "fighting stance" (which comes so easily to those who train in martial arts). You start with your hands held loosely together below your waist and only raise them if you feel your boundaries are threatened.

Even then you are told categorically not to point or look like you are pointing, so you keep your hands with the palms facing forwards. Language is crucial and swearing a BIG no-no. The question "What do you want?" is designed to make an aggressor actually think of a response involving what is known as higher brain function as they have to consider their response.

We were encouraged to utilise the phrases "You need to leave!" and "Back away!" or Back off!" when dealing with threatening or intimidating behaviour.

There were two groups with a coach and several "woofers" on designated areas of the sports hall. One at a time we went out onto the mats and had to deal with them. The guys we were facing wore sunglasses so you couldn't see their eyes, further upping the adrenaline factor and their behaviour towards us ranged from mildly obnoxious to criminally aggressive.

In order to enhance the realism of the role plays, the actors would pick up on personal traits or clothing choices. I wear bandanas to keep my hair out of my face in training and that day was wearing a camouflage patterned one. Sure enough, the opening line as they pounded towards me was "You in the army or something?!!" When I replied "Sorry mate, I can't hear you" the guy snarled and went "WHAT YOU DEAF AS WELL?!! AND I'M NOT YOUR F***ING MATE!!!" Heart hammering in my chest I stuck to the game plan, while coach Caroline Braxton stood behind me observing what was going on. I shouted "BACK AWAY!!! JUST GO!!! LEAVE!!!" and various combinations while the actors continued to make fun of me but did back off. There was one practitioner from my club Krav Maga Midlands was there and it was good to have a team mate on board.

As the others went up it was clear that the actors wouldn't back away unless we ticked certain boxes with regard to etiquette on our own behalf. Anyone pointing (a gesture infuriatingly easy to make when your hands are outstretched) would have the actors yelling indignantly at them and coming back. Anyone who walked towards them (again, an easy mistake to make) would be perceived as "wanting some". Finally we all went through the drills and during a short lunch break I spoke to FAST UK Director Wayne Hubball and Caroline Braxton.

Wayne said, "It's gone very well. Everyone seems to have picked up all the learning points. It's great to see how people have advanced from Adrenaline 1."

Caroline is also a specialist in Neuro Linguistic Programming and incorporating FAST into corporate business. She said, "I think it's going really, really well.

The training's embedded in them and while you all might not remember what you did in Adrenaline 1, it's all coming back. It's a nice recap."

After lunch Jon Bullock then took us for what could euphemistically be called a "warm up". We worked on trying to get our partners to the floor; punching to the body; groups of 3 with two vs. one and several variations. Jon told us on several occasions not to "pretend" about what we were doing and to deal with our movements realistically. This went on for about 40 minutes and was about as grueling as my last Krav Maga grading. Afterwards Jon stated that while we might hate him at that moment he had done us a favour by "inoculating" us to what we were about to do and also getting us used to being in close quarters brawling. He also pointed out that the biggest fear we really had was not of getting hurt but of failing, or looking foolish in front of our friends and peers.

Then it came time to meet the predators again. The last time I faced these guys I was beyond nervous. This time I was enthusiastic but there was no way of denying that the nerves were jangling once more. We split into two groups of roughly 25 people, with a coach and several predators per group. The students lined up facing each other either side of the squares, and each line took turns. The worst part about this is the initial phase, where you stand, usually with your back to the predators and close your eyes. You inform the coach of any niggling injuries (in my case a dodgy left knee) and she will signal to them which bit of your body they should try to avoid hurting. Then the game's on.

The first time I was up, I got violently shoved forwards and whirled to find a guy stood behind me, shouting incoherent threats and trying to slap and push me.

His mates were also marching up and then I was retaliating. You have no chance to try and remember what techniques you may have learned in Krav or any other discipline, you are operating solely on instinct and muscle memory. The whole thing was a blur that retrospectively seemed to last about 2 seconds. I remember using an elbow strike to knock one opponent on his back and that was about it. Before I knew it the whistle was blowing and it was all over, people clapping, and me trying to get my breath back.

It was interesting to see how different people handled the situations. Some of the better fighters really made their punches and kicks count while the most aggressive fighters in these situations appeared to be the women.

After a short break for the predators to breathe, we went up once more. The second time I had a rougher deal with one guy pinning my arms. I was screaming a lot of abuse and dropping clusters of C-bombs while Caroline encouraged me to yell at them. One or two of the other guys who went up had opportunities to use verbal "persuasion" rather than just punching, proving the point that if you are trained to handle adrenaline you can react appropriately. Another thing that happened four or five times was guys losing their T-shirts while grappling. The predators would take advantage of this and try and keep it over the practitioner's face unless they managed to wriggle free.

Our side of the room finished before the other and we joined the remaining group to give them some encouragement. Amusingly, the predators from our side then joined in, meaning some guys had to fight up to five at a time. Finally we stopped and Andras Millward gave a closing talk followed by Jon Bullock who asked us how we felt the day had gone and got us to give a round of applause to the "crazy guys" who donned the Predator armour. We then got our attendance certificates and shook Andras's hand before changing into fresh T-shirts and anticipating a good meal and a shower.

I spoke to Andras Millward again who said, "I love doing these events with KMG. You guys come in with full commitment and honesty and it makes our job a lot easier. You really bring your heart and soul into every fight. In the grey areas of verbal assertion you guys are really good. A lot of you handled some very, very complex scenarios."

Jon Bullock was also very pleased with how things had gone.

"The idea was obviously to give them the adrenaline experience again. What we did this time was change the dynamic. So there's pressure but there's more things to think about such as movement, positioning, dealing with more than one person. It is likely that in general a self defence situation would involve more than one person."

I asked him to sum up the day in three words and he replied, "Experience, learning, and review."

A great day for everyone involved. The predators, coaches, instructors and students all had a great time and I cannot speak highly enough of this event. Adrenaline is just what I needed. I am now looking forward to getting more involved in this world and the future is bright.

**Brace Yourself**

21st June 2015

I have a snapped ACL (anterior crusciate ligament) in my left knee. It broke in 2001 and I've never had it repaired...but this year I finally will. It aches when I train in Krav and unless I wear not one but two elasticated supports on it, it will sometimes swell like a balloon and hurt like a bitch the next day. I can't go running (advice of a sports masseur/ knee specialist) and flexibility on that leg is piss poor (kicks to anywhere higher than an opponent's belly button are in the realms of fantasy). I have always regarded this injury as debilitating and something that has affected my ability to be fully effective in both Krav and the rest of my life. Last week I flew to Crete for 4 weeks holiday and made doubly certain that I packed BOTH knee supports for when I go to join Krav Maga Chania, a club on the island who have invited me to train with them.

Today I was hanging out at the beach with a few pals and got introduced to an Australian girl with a broken foot. I initially believed that her foot HAD BEEN broken and now had healed...but was probably still a bit sore.

Turns out that her foot was STILL broken and was in the process of healing. She had come to the beach with her pals, but as its access is via a rocky cliff face only...she had gone to the neighbouring beach and then swum round to join her mates....who had carried her foot brace in a bag for her. Already impressed by this I was even more inspired when she swam back round as we were leaving, rendezvoused with us at the top of the drive leading to both beaches.

She strapped on her brace and then clopped off down the road...at a pace slightly faster than my normal "On Holiday Stroll."

She snorted at the idea of taking a cab from the taverna 10 minutes further down the road and after we'd stopped there for lunch we walked back along a trail that required climbing fences, navigating goat paths and walking through olive groves. She didn't moan or complain once and when I asked if the brace didn't sweat a bit, she replied that it came with a sock but she'd stopped wearing it and that it now "chafed a bit" but didn't elaborate further.

On the final stretch of the walk home she asked where a good bar with dancing could be found and also a decent beach for snorkeling. She added that it should be relatively close to Plakias but only because her foot meant she was limited in range.

Meeting her today has made me realise that a LOT of what's holding me back is not actual injury or obstacles but my perception of them. While I'm not so bendy on my left side any more my main worry in training is what MIGHT happen due to the ACL being in tatters...not the fact that it actually is.

## Krav Maga Chania: Part 1

28th June 2015

My father retired out to Crete in about 1997 and for the last few years I have paid him a visit in the summers, having a wonderful yet usually booze-fuelled time in the sun kissed, beach paradise that is Plakias.

Last year I thought about training with a Greek Krav club while on holiday but the nearest one was on the mainland in Athens.

This year I was more fortunate as Dimitris Kontekakis recently converted from Pure Krav Maga to KMG in November 2014. His club has about 50 members, including a small kickboxing club and a junior Krav Maga club of children. When I contacted him he was more than happy at my suggestion that I pay him and a visit to train with them.

Plakias is fairly isolated and about 60km from Chania so I planned out getting there the day before and also laid off the beer in preparation for Kravving abroad. It took two buses to get to the city and when I rolled in, the hotel was a pleasant walk from the coach station and I checked in before phoning Dimitris to touch base. He offered to pick me up on his motorbike about 8.30pm and advised me to chill out with a coffee and get something to eat.

When he arrived to pick me up I think it's the first time I've had an in depth conversation about Krav Maga, while riding through the streets of a city on the back of a motorbike. We got to the club to see some guys already there, stretching and warming up. The heat was strong, which I assumed was the reason for the late start time, and even with two ceiling fans, the heat was something I knew I'd need to try and manage.

After being introduced to everyone I got changed and we lined up for the initial Kida. We did some group warming up and more of the ever necessary stretching and then Dimitris formally introduced me to everyone and said that out of respect for "our guest" the lesson would be conducted in English, with him speaking in Greek after for the students who didn't understand it. This was decent of him as I'd imagined he would translate for me, not the other way round. Dimitris then said we would be working on blocking kicks, covering most types of both kick and defence and said he would appreciate my feedback on anything I felt like adding to the mix.

We worked as both attackers and defenders and despite going "light" during the drills (I had left my shin guards at home) me and my partner banged bones a couple of times and were hopping about, silently cursing.

I was finding the heat in the room oppressive but as we hadn't been told to take a water break, and no one else had asked to, I was determined not to be the first to ask. After about 30 minutes Dimitris told everyone to get a drink and I chugged about half a litre. I then jokingly mentioned not wanting to "wimp out" and, in the spirit of true Krav Maga common sense, he told me that I should have done as I wasn't used to training in this heat.

We moved on to blocking stomp kicks with arms and hands, and he used my wonky finger (from incorrectly blocking a kick in training with an open hand last October), to warn the others of the necessity of correct technique.

We switched to striking focus mitts, with a group of 6 in the middle and another half dozen guys holding the pads in a circle. You had to go full out on the pads with the guy holding them dictating what strikes were required by changing positions.

After this we had a pressure drill doing choke hold releases...but with the added twist of it being in the dark with the lights off. I hadn't tried this before and it got the adrenalin flowing to be fighting with shadows while INXS's "Suicide Blonde" was playing loudly over the gym's stereo to further up the mood factor.

Finally we moved on to some bag work to wind down, and then lined up for the final Kida. I was soaking wet with sweat and so tired that I was rummaging in my backpack for the Krav Maga Midlands T-shirt I'd brought as a gift, that it took 2 minutes before I realised it was someone else's bag. Finally locating it I handed it to Dimitris who grinned and said "I have one for you, but you beat me to it."

He then invited me back in 2 weeks to train again and have a meal with him and the club.

So...I get to do this again in a fortnight.

Watch this space.

## Krav Maga Chania: Part 2

### 15th July 2015

After a great time with Dimitris and his club in Chania, Crete on 24th June I was more than keen to go back for another session. The turmoil of the possible Grexit from Europe had been going on for a few weeks but despite the gloomy pessimism on Facebook the only obvious sign of impending isolation from the Eurozone was huge queues of anxious tourists at the cash points.

I came back 4 days before the end of my holiday and caught a lift with Manolis, a former Brit who'd moved to Crete as a child. A lot of the guys were already there warming up as we arrived and Dimitris was enthusiastic, shaking my hand and telling me all about his time doing the KMG Combat Mindset & Mental Conditioning Course in Israel the previous week. The youngest member of the club Mirto was celebrating her 17th birthday and had decided to train anyway. Emmanouhl, another practitioner also had his birthday so there were lots of cakes and soda laid out ready for afterwards, a sight for sore eyes and something to look forward to, for any practitioner after a heavy session.

After the last time where I had excruciating muscle cramps for most of the night following the training, I had taken advice from people I trust, and glugged down about 3 litres of water and eaten well during the day. Apparently it's not replenishment after training that counts but what you put in beforehand. Your body loses vital fluids and replacement takes time. The temperature in the gym was again around the 30 degrees Celsius mark and I had no desire to be doing the Ministry of Silly Walks around my hotel room while stifling screams at 4am again.

We warmed up with the usual stretches and running then moved on to the introductions on my behalf to the club members who weren't there last time. We did some striking work on the pads and bags around the walls of the gym and then we shifted to a work through of the techniques used to escape from choke holds.

This proved useful and at Krav Maga Midlands back home, I had done a lot of this drilling. After various methods were gone through Dimitris then demonstrated one I hadn't seen before. He got a student to choke him with his head up close and no room to maneuver, the attacker's body pressed up against him. He then grabbed the guys head and mimed twisting it to the side.

This would hurt like hell in a real situation and when I was asked for my feedback I pointed out that the technique I'd been taught was to lower your body weight, adjust your stance to balance and then force the assailant's head backwards, preferably while thumbing their eye sockets. Dimitris agreed that this was the established technique but added that this method was for if the person had got too close for you to be able to effectively utilise that defence.

After my misplaced machismo over water breaks last time I made certain I was hydrated throughout the class and got through 2 bottles by the time it was over.

Afterwards we had a small party at the club for Mirto and Manolis before heading out to a taverna for dinner. This was a really nice way to round off the training and I had a good chat with Dimitris and club member Lefteris who had given me a lift to the restaurant. Dimitris hadn't heard of Fast Defence and was intrigued by the video I showed him of the Adrenaline 2 event in June. He quickly got in touch with Wayne Hubball via Facebook with a view to finding out more. I suggested that next summer some more guys from KMM come over to train with him and he was more than up for it. After a lovely Greek dinner including a huge steak (not to mention a good few glasses of cold beer) we said goodbye and I headed back to my hotel.

Really great time on the two sessions and it was a privilege to see another country's KMG club and to train with these guys. Can't wait to go back again and my thanks to Dimitris and all the guys at KMC who made this such a great experience.

Efcharistó

## Night Parks 5: The Robbery
## RSC Park, Stratford upon Avon, UK

17th July 2015

KMM run the Night Parks seminar once a year in mid to late summer. This was my 3rd one, with the previous editions focusing on protecting third parties and how to deal with spontaneous violence and the threat of harm.

This time the focus was on robbery, with guns and knives taking centre stage and much less emphasis on protecting other people. We were going straight for the jugular, with some brutal techniques and takedowns.

I got there about 6.30pm. After a while the rest of the guys turned up, including one from Total Krav Maga in Thames Valley who had also joined us for Warzone 2 last year. After a quick warm up and some funny looks off passers by, we moved into techniques involving being threatened with knives.

By coincidence, on the same day of the seminar, new laws came into force in the UK that make it a much more serious offence to be caught illegally carrying a bladed weapon in public. Those caught for a second time by the police now face a mandatory 6 months minimum term in prison. Knife crime, and in particular robberies and sexual assaults have risen by 10% in the last 4 years in the UK.

Bartosz made it very clear that the best thing to do in any situation is to comply with a robber who simply wants your money, especially if they are right up against you.

He acted out several scenarios with Russell where he handed over some money but dropped it on the floor to distract the assailant, enabling enough of a distraction so he could run away.

He emphasised that splitting is THE most important thing to do because if you linger, then the robber may want more. Him and Russ then amusingly acted out Russell wanting more and more until he eventually led Bartosz away saying "Let's go and find your car."

We then partnered off and moved through various positions to approach a victim with verbal threats being used. We were shown how to both deflect and disarm as well as compliance followed by scarpering out of the danger zone.

After a good workout with the training knives, we then moved on to guns. These are bright yellow for the simple reason that it makes it glaringly obvious they're not real. Russell recounted a story of the police armed response unit being called to deal with his friend who was playing with a BB gun in the garden.

The techniques for gun disarms are something we'd done before but a new addition to the repertoire was grabbing a gun from someone who's gesturing with it near your body in unpredictable patterns. Something I learned a LONG time ago is that you always keep your finger way clear of the trigger guard, even on a bendy, banana coloured replica pistol, unless you want to be howling all the way to A&E in the back of an ambulance, cradling a broken index finger.

As the sun began to go down we finally moved on to what Bartosz always calls "the fun bit" but we call the Tunnel of Love. Next to the river in the park is a pathway with bushes and tress either side. Perfect for a multiple attackers scenario...especially in the dark.

Unlike last year we didn't go through with a partner to "protect" but instead had to navigate the walkway on our own. A Go-Pro camera had been purchased since the last seminar and also a chest harness so the first guy through was wearing that. The last two seminars, we'd been given specific tasks by Bartosz but he told us to improvise and alternate between sticks, knives, guns and simply being innocent people who either wanted a chat or to ask the time. He made it clear that anyone not in grabbing range of a gun who refused to obey a gunman's instructions would get push ups as a penance. This emphasised the importance of safety rather than heroics that may fail and get you killed.

I was second one up and even though I've done both this type of thing before plus Wayne Hubball's Adrenaline it always gets the blood flowing and the fear factor high. A camera flash went off while I was trying to negotiate my way past two bad guys and the next thing I knew one had 'stabbed' me to death. Moving on I had people wanting a hug, trying to persuade me to have a threesome with them and another woman, and a guy who simply took a flying kick at me. Finally making it through, I had the usual amnesia over 80% of the journey but was told I'd handled it all well.

As people went through it was interesting to watch the different personalities and methods. One guy lashed out at everyone who approached him, even when four of us simply asked him the time. Bartosz was following him through shouting "They're not attacking you!" but got no response. This proved just how wired it is possible to get in this type of situation and the "blinkers" will come on, causing tunnel vision to threats. When one lad, a former Olympic wrestler, came through Russell stood as River Bank Monitor to the side. This was in case anyone got thrown, rag doll fashion into the cold waters of the Avon.

When one lady was in the tunnel I held my arms out as if to give her a hug but then cuffed the side of her face with my hand. She instantly responded with a dig to my left eye, which sent my contact lens to the bank and had me backing off. Goz Gozwell was her usual feisty self, not giving ground and screaming her head off at anyone who got in her face.

Finally we all got through and lined up on the grass for feedback. One very valid point raised was that there were a lot of passers by who could hear what we were doing, who did not know WHY we were doing it but had made NO attempt to either intervene or call the police. This proved that you need to be self reliant in situations like this in real life, and not assume that help will be there.

After a few words from each of us about how we felt we then did the final kida and moved to the Dirty Duck pub for a well earned pint.

As usual, top notch training and the added treat of the Tunnel of Love at the end to test everyone's muscle memory, resilience and "courage under fire".

## Adrenaline 3: Room 101
## Unique Results Personal Training & Fitness Centre
## Chelmsford, Essex

10th August 2015

The final of three courses, tailored for Krav Maga Global UK by Wayne Hubball and his team at FAST Reality UK. Adrenaline 1 focused on dealing, both verbally and physically, with one aggressor. Level 2 thrust students into scenarios with between two and six attackers. Level 3 however, was a sequel in name only.

By invitation, with 10 applicants being refused attendance, this took things to not only a new level but a newly built level, a level created specially for us. Inspired by Rory Miller, Adrenaline 3 was the equivalent of room 101 from George Orwell's novel '1984'. Working through your own personal demons. Stand and face what you are most afraid of. Your fears and darkest dreads. No place to hide.

I got to the gym at about 8.30am to find Wayne and Jon Bullock, head of KMG UK in the car park with FAST's Dr Kirsty Hunter along with FAST instructors Alan Dennis and Fraser Bishop. The kick off was set for 9 o'clock and guys began to arrive and fill up the lecture room we were going to use for the first part of the day. The 'theory" side was set to take up a lot more than on the previous sessions, mainly due to the much more immersive nature this time. There were 25 of us and one Krav Maga instructor had flown over from Norway, arriving that morning and flying home the same day. It was good to see familiar faces from several clubs.

I spoke to a lad from Krav Maga JW3 in London. He said: "I'm quite interested in the flinch response training, the in-fight decision making. I've realised how important it is, especially when dealing with multiple attackers."

I got a word with Wayne Hubball too. He told me: "I'm looking forward to all these guys that have come on Adrenaline 1 and Adrenaline 2 moving into the next level and giving them a greater understanding of making decisions under pressure. Not just going out and being aggressive but also the difference between high brain and low brain and making the right decisions."

After a cup of coffee and some introductions we were greeted by Jon who said he was very pleased at the enthusiasm we'd showed but pointed out that this was going to be poles apart from what had gone before. A mindset of being willing to learn and having self control were pre-requisites. He further elaborated on why he'd rejected ten people from levels 1 and 2 who'd requested to attend as he did not feel they were suitable for the event.

Dr Hunter, FAST's Head of Science then gave a lecture

on the science of making decisions under threat and we were introduced to Fraser Bishop, a former Metropolitan police firearms officer. He told us about the legal rights we have as civilians to use violence and in particular focused upon section 76 of the Criminal Justice and Immigration Act 2008. This covers what is 'reasonable force" for the purposes of self defence.

After the introductory lectures we then broke for a few minutes and headed over to the main sports hall. I got a quick word with Jon about what the day was going to involve. "I'm looking to consolidate all the learning and adrenaline from 1 and 2 in a more personalised, scenario based experience.

People understanding decisions such as when they may or may not need to engage in conflict. The fact that self defence on the street really does have no rules and to train to as close to 'no rules' as possible. Keep us thinking outside of our training bias, what we think works, what doesn't work, what's our favourite, what we like to do, how we expect the person to react even if they don't react in that way. As close to the unknown as possible. Combine that with the aspects of how the brain works. Also the legal use of force. Put you in a situation where you have to make a decision based on all of those factors and have an outcome that you will then review. This will hopefully prepare you for real life, the real world."

When we got into our groin guards and gym clothes the initial warm up was intense, my greatest memory being the "elbows pointing in" push ups that really put strain on the muscles. We then went to pair work and a unique form of slow fighting that I'd never seen before called Range Rover from Tony Blauer, a close quarter tactics specialist. Jon demonstrated with two Krav Maga students from Elite, that one will call out a command from a list such as 'Grapple', 'Kick', 'Close' or 'Punch' and their partner had to obey that command and react as if hit. Then the other person gave a command. The purpose of this was to see if people would rely on the moves and strikes they were comfortable with or strongest at. It was very odd trying to adapt to this but it proved to all of us that we will 99% of the time favour what we know works, even if that means going off balance or leaving vulnerable areas unprotected. We moved to heavy fighting, involving grappling and a stipulation that "there are no rules". Jon encouraged us to do whatever we felt was necessary to get the upper hand. We were about to start when my partner was swapped for a small woman who I'd seen at Adrenaline 2 and I knew was a ferocious scrapper.

When we went to it I was stronger and managed to get her down on the ground but holding her there proved to be another world entirely. I couldn't pin her and when we stopped and took a quick breather before changing partners I was already getting knackered. Jon encouraged us to choose a partner "that you're most afraid of" so I chose a bloke who is a lot bigger than me and very strong. When we started fighting I kept him at a distance by repeatedly kicking his shins.

After, we split up into groups of five. Jon told us to number off from 1 to 5 and to tell the others some information about ourselves that would be written down by another group mate. Within this we were asked to reveal something that we are afraid of or that makes us feel uncomfortable. Jon stressed not to go too far and only share as much as we were comfortable with. I was number 1 and spoke about how, as a child, I'd been overheard talking in my sleep, shouting as if being surrounded and hemmed in, with cries of "GET OFF! LEAVE ME ALONE! JUST GO AWAY!" My father had always said it sounded like I was surrounded and being threatened by people out to hurt me. I then moved to the back of the room while the other four in my group decided what scenario they would like me to face. We were told that we could use each other as actors, other people from the other groups if need be, and also both Wayne and Fraser who would be in full Predator armour. Numbers 2 to 5 then went through the same routines and finally everyone had handed in their slips of paper and we were ready to go. Dr Hunter spoke to us in final preparation and said that if we wanted to wear heart rate monitors during our scenarios then we could, and the results would track the before, during, and after of the events.

Me and the other 1's then went 'backstage' to the next room and a crash mat was placed over the entrance as an impromptu door, so we couldn't see the others preparing.

My nerves were on edge when Alan Dennis came to join us and handed out torso impact armour (imagine SWAT bullet proof vests but without the Kevlar) and boxing helmets. This was clearly going to be a lot more intense than Adrenaline 1 or 2, where we'd worn nothing protective except groin shields. As we kitted up Jon came to summon the first person and her scenario began. We weren't allowed to watch but the snippets of conversation I overheard involved Wayne using some foul language towards her, albeit in a controlled manner, and accusing her of being aggressive. The set piece ended without getting physical and after the student had had a debrief with Dr Hunter she told me that the set-up involved her boss threatening to sack her unless she 'did what he asked' and being physically oppressive during the encounter. She had remained calm and simply refused, resulting in getting 'fired'. She told me that she'd wanted to "kick him in the bollocks" but had kept her cool. More guys went in and all of these went to physical altercations.

Then it was my turn.

Jon came to get me and said that the words "Start scenario" would initiate the role play, with "End scenario" concluding it. He informed me that I was a postman (my current day job) out delivering mail and to chat to anyone I saw and just act as if everything was normal. As I stepped onto the mats I was met by a woman who cheerfully asked if she could have a parcel as she was going out. This happens sometimes when I'm on delivery in real life, and the answer has to be 'no' unless you actually know the person by sight. I politely refused but then saw both 'Predators' and about three other guys walking towards me slowly, like something out of The Walking Dead. As I tried to move away they surrounded me and I could hear angry remarks and someone shouting "Just give her the f***ing package!"

Hemmed in against the wall I could feel the rush of adrenaline and punched the Predator in front of me in the 'face'. Next thing they were all over me, shouting at each other to hurt me and get me down on the floor. I tried grappling with one Predator but he threw me down by my neck. It was only later when I saw the video of the fight that I realised just how much adrenaline, fear and stress can distort memory. I would have sworn that I was dogpiled by some or all of the group but on film it's only Wayne Hubball in Predator gear on top of me. I managed to struggle to my feet, punched Fraser's Predator a final and then legged it off the mats, hearing Jon saying "End scenario" and people clapping.

In the debrief Dr Hunter asked how I felt and to be honest I could feel the panic rising and ebbing in my chest as I sat facing her. This had been WAY different to my previous experiences with Adrenaline and Garry Stacey who had gone out just before me was nearby, saying he felt the same way. The scenario had targeted a very basic childhood fear, a fear of being surrounded and attacked. Worst of all the 'assault' was unprovoked and I felt I had done nothing to warrant the kicking they were trying to give me. I asked Dr Hunter how she thought I'd done and she gave me a look as if to say "Seriously?" When I just looked at her silently she then added "You did very well, you didn't give up and got out. Well done."

As the other guys went through one at a time, it was fascinating to see the inventiveness of some scenarios and how they reacted. One lad from KMM had a scenario involving a woman being threatened by the Predators.

He intervened and went hands on with them but said afterwards that this had awakened a very basic and cultural need within him as a Russian man to protect a woman in danger, even if it meant harm to himself. He added that he was amazed at how his self control had dissolved whereas on Adrenaline 1 and 2 he had kept his cool. He told me later:

"There were no fear as such, interestingly. They somehow triggered a protection response – a fear that I will be not be able to protect someone I care about. They could not have known it – I definitely did not mention it and did not even think about it."

One scenario involved ensuring the safety of children when faced by multiple opponents such as an abduction and the student went full on with both Predators, losing his mask in the process but continuing to fight until "End scenario" was called. What was interesting was his reflection on whether taking the scenario physical was indeed, the safest or best choice?.

One participant stands well over 6'3" feet tall and is a big guy yet very mild mannered. His scenario was that his 'daughter' (played by a female student) was having an argument with her boyfriend (Fraser in Predator gear). The twist was that it was set in the student's house. After stepping on the mats the woman said "Leave it Dad, I'll deal with it" but the Predator was verbally aggressive. He got in between them and gave the guy two or three warnings to back off and let him talk to his daughter.

To everyone's surprise, when the last warning was ignored he simply picked the Predator up by the back of his torso armour and groin guard and virtually carried him off the mats with the words, "You've been told to do something. You said no. You're in my house so out you go!" and pushed him out of the 'room'.

Much laughter from the rest of us but it showed the protective instinct very well. Imagine Liam Neeson from the movie Taken, but in MMA gear.

Later scenarios involved a lady being sexually harassed and asking the woman who was in the scenario to help her. Others included neighbours complaining about babies crying (to a student with a baby son in real life); a bar manager attempting to remove drunk and verbally abusive patrons; and a father hysterically searching for his lost baby. Another had all of us on the mats pretending to be drunk, loud yet friendly football fans who were greeting the guy and his 'family' (actors playing his wife and daughter) by surrounding them and singing but not actually making threats. He simply left, politely shaking his head and smiling and said afterwards that he was desperate to protect the people he was with but realised quickly that we didn't mean him any harm. He added that throwing punches would have been counter productive as he was greatly outnumbered anyway. The words "End scenario" would not be spoken unless either the student managed to get away or alternatively deal with the situation satisfactorily (such as the first one, involving attempted coercion into giving sexual favours for career advancement). As Jon said later, it was the student who created the end.

Finally we moved through everyone and then sat with Jon, Wayne, Alan, Fraser and Kirsty for the feedback. Jon pointed out that whole aim of training was that the least creative solution is the safest. A surprise to most of us was the revelation that scenarios had only got physical if the person made it so or didn't take a decision early enough to avoid it going physical. In my scenario, had I simply shouted straight away "NOT IN THE MOOD GUYS!" and walked off, then they would never have mobbed me.

By punching the Predator I had given the gang facing me a licence to attack.

Wayne and Jon elaborated that the first two Adrenaline events were about how the body responds when the heart rate goes up. Now we understood that, the idea was to create scenarios based on making decisions under stress and above all to try and avoid, if possible, going to conflict. Many factors had, in my opinion, contributed to our mindset of needing to go hands-on. From being given a torso shield and helmet (implying that things would almost certainly get physical) to our previous experiences at Adrenaline events and in Krav Maga training. Finally they rounded up by saying that no decision made that day in the scenarios was wrong or judged it was simply what we did at the time. We all gave a short opinion on how we felt the day had gone and what we'd learned.

I said that my set-piece had awakened some unpleasant

memories and feelings but that going out of my comfort zone like this meant I was now more at peace with some personal demons. Once everyone had spoken, Kirsty gave her views, saying just how thrilled she was to work with KMG students as we always "give it 100%" and it was a pleasure to be there with us.

Jon then reminded us that Adrenaline with KMG in its current format was now over and presented us with special T-shirts for having attended events 1 to 3 and then a certificate of attendance. A couple of photos of us all and we made our way home.

Tremendous day and working with fear, particularly deep rooted fear like we did was a unique yet unsettling and ultimately rewarding experience.

I cannot sing the praises of this type of training highly enough and look forward to training with Adrenaline and FAST Reality a lot more in the future.

**Thanks to:**

Bartosz, Russell and Al- Krav Maga Midlands instructors.

Jon Bullock, KMG UK Director.

Anna Surowiec- Active Krav Maga chief instructor.

Goz Gozwell, Viesturs Vavere and Lewis Turpin.

Eyal Yanilov

Zeev Cohen

Rune Lind

The kids and parents at Junior Safe Krav Maga

Coro Ellis

Wayne Hubball- Director, FAST Reality

Marco Zanitzer & Daniele Stazi and all at Krav Maga Roma, Italy

Dimitris Kontekakis and all at Krav Maga Chania, Crete

Ken Garriques, E2- Krav Maga Bristol City Centre

Cover image courtesy of Iamnee at FreeDigitalPhotos.net

Printed in Great Britain
by Amazon